# The Amelia Earhart Saga: Plausible Suppositions

# Barry W. Bower

Suzanne Bower
2015

~ ⌣

# About the Author

Barry Wayne Bower was born in Rochester, New York in 1932. After graduation from High School in Leroy, New York, he enrolled for undergraduate and graduate work at the State of University of New York at Geneseo where he received a B.S. in Elementary Education and a M.S. in Science in Elementary Education.

After serving in the Army and teaching junior and senior mathematics at Clarence Central Schools in Clarence, New York, he joined the Marketing Division of the Scott-Foresman Publishing Company.

Retiring from Scott-Foresman in 1990, he moved to Batavia, New York where he was involved in a variety of community activities, including serving on the City Council, working on the 1993 Buffalo World University Games, the Wings of Eagles Air Shows, the National Junior College Division III Baseball World Series and serving many years as Chairman of the Batavia Recreational Corporation.

After moving to Hanover, Pennsylvania in 2007 he joined the Rotary Club and served as an election clerk.

Barry began six years of extensive research on Earhart, amassing boxes of file folders on Earhart's life after July 2, 1937.

Fortunately, he had a first draft of the book completed when he entered the hospital for surgery on September 30, 2014. Tragically, he passed away on October 22, 2014, with his last wish being to have his book published. Thus, his family and friends began to carry out this desire.

© 2015 Suzanne Bower. All Rights Reserved.

The Amelia Earhart Saga: Plausible Suppositions
Bower, Barry W.

No part of this book may be reproduced in any written, electronic, recording, or photocopying without written permission of the publisher or author. The exception would be in the case of brief quotations embodied in the critical articles or reviews and pages where permission is specifically granted by the publisher or author.

ISBN: 978-0-578-16567-7
Library of Congress Control Number: 2015944847
First Edition Printed in the United States

# DEDICATION

This book is dedicated to you, Amelia Mary Earhart in remembrance of your aeronautical achievements. Your life after July 2, 1937 was not what you could have ever imagined.

# ACKNOWLEDGEMENTS

I would like to thank my wife Suzanne for her patience and understanding while I was writing this book and after I was no longer able to actively participate with this venture. To our daughters Wendy and Lynn who were also supportive of the project, my sincere appreciation. I would also like to thank my granddaughter Jennifer who used her skills to hone the original drafts into a readable manuscript before the final version was sent to the printer.

Many fellow researchers contributed their thoughts and ideas to this manuscript. In most cases, their contributions are recognized in the text. And to my friend Bill Brown, thank you for your wonderful guidance and support.

# CONTENTS

# INTRODUCTION

This is my story of Amelia Earhart, whose record-setting exploits earned her world-renowned recognition. I have always been interested in Amelia Earhart being a pilot myself but my desire to find out what really happened to her that fateful day elevated after visiting a local YMCA. Strange I know and some may think I'm crazy but we all have had experiences where something has spoken to us from the beyond or have had a déjà vu moment. As I was about to leave the YMCA I happened to notice a picture of Amelia Earhart on a bulletin board in the lobby. At that moment I started to get that weird feeling I was being asked to continue my peaked interest in Amelia.

I immediately went home and began doing my research. I read just about every book possible, looked at several maps, including planning out her flight and talked to numerous fellow researchers. After years of dedicating myself to finding out the truth, I have finally been able to put everything on paper for you to read. The following chapters are my own beliefs and conclusions and you can take them as you wish. My only desire is that you at least think about what is being said, you can continue to believe what I have written is true or walk away. But it is up to you as the reader to think what you want.

# 1 AMELIA MARY EARHART

Amelia Mary Earhart, one of America's most famous heroines was born in Atchison, Kansas on July 24, 1897. Amy Otis Earhart, the daughter of a prominent Kansas Judge, had been raised according to the standards of the wealthy.

Amelia's father Edwin was a struggling attorney for the railroads. He felt pressure from Judge Otis, his father-in-law, who expected him to provide for his family in the fashion to which his daughter Amy had been accustomed to.

He and his family, now including a second daughter Muriel, moved around while he worked at several different jobs. They lived in a number of cities including Des Moines, St. Paul and Chicago, where Amelia graduated from Hyde Park High School in 1915. She then attended Ogontz, a finishing school in the suburbs of Philadelphia. Leaving in the middle of her second year, she worked as a nurse's aid in a military hospital in Toronto, Canada; tending to the wounded from World War I. After that, she enrolled at Columbia College in New York City to study medicine. She soon lost interest in that and moved to Los Angeles to be with her family.

On January 3, 1921, Amelia took her first flying lesson from Neta Snook and six months later purchased her first airplane, a used Kinner Airster. Since the biplane was painted yellow, she named it *The Canary* and flew it to set her first flight record on October 22, 1922 by climbing to 14,000 feet.

Leaving California in 1924 with her mother as a passenger, she motored to the east coast and took a job as a social worker at the Dennison House in Boston. In April 1928, a call from Hilton Railey on behalf of George Palmer Putnam, book publisher and publicist changed her life. He asked if she would like to be the first woman to fly the Atlantic Ocean and her immediate response was, "Yes." At an interview in New York City, she met Putnam, who took a special interest in her. Thus, on June 17, 1928, she climbed aboard a Fokker F-7 named *Friendship* with pilot Wilmer "Bill" Stultz and co-pilot/mechanic Louis E. "Slim" Gordon. With Amelia as a passenger, the tri-motored aircraft lifted off from Trepassey Harbor, Newfoundland, crossed the Atlantic in 20 hours and 40 minutes and landed offshore at Burry Port, Wales. That landmark flight made headlines worldwide. Although Amelia received most of the accolades, she told friends that she had felt like a "sack of potatoes" because she never once was allowed to fly the airplane.

The three who had been aboard the *Friendship* when it crossed the Atlantic were driven in a tickertape parade in New York and were received by President Calvin Coolidge at a White House reception. The *Friendship* was returned to LeRoy, New York, by its owner Donald Woodward in time for the October 12, 1928 opening of his airport; which was considered the finest private airport in the nation. Amelia visited that airport on January 24, 1929, saw the *Friendship* for the first time since the Atlantic flight and met its owner.

Since the oceanic flight, Amelia's aviation career had escalated, which was helped immensely by a man she would eventually call GP and reluctantly agree to marry in 1932. Her record flights included those for speed, distance and altitude. She helped organize the Ninety Nines, an airline, lectured throughout the United States and wrote books. Two solo oceanic flights would bring lasting fame. She flew a Lockheed Vega across the Atlantic in May 1932 and from Hawaii to California in January 1935.

Amelia's unfinished world flight, however, has kept her name in the headlines since July 2, 1937. She and navigator Fred Noonan left Lae, New Guinea in a Lockheed Electra 10E, which never arrived at Howland Island. That disappearance, including all its ramification and theories has caused thousands of researchers to seek the truth about what really began that fateful day.

3

# 2    JAPANESE PLANS

On July 26, 1777, George Washington, General and Commander in Chief of the Continental Army, declared, "The necessity of procuring good intelligence is apparent and need not to be further discussed." W.E.B. Griffin and William J. Butterworth used that quote in the opening of their book, *The Outlaws: A Presidential Agent Novel*. In *Roosevelt's Secret War*, Joseph E. Persico wrote "Espionage involves peeking at the other fellow's hand, cooking the books, poisoning the well, breaking the rules, hitting below the belt, cheating, lying, deceiving, defaming, snooping, eavesdropping, prying, stealing, bribing, suborning, burglarizing, forcing, misleading, conducting dirty tricks, dirty pool, skullduggery, blackmail, deduction, everything not sporting, not kosher and not cricket."

When Japan invaded China in 1937, the United States was clinging to a tenuous peace. Soon after World War I, Congress had passed a law that no Government agency could do intelligence gathering outside the borders of the United States. With the Atlantic and Pacific to protect the country, no further entanglements in foreign wars was wanted. In 1925, Secretary of State Henry Stimson, poorly informed and naively idealistic, declared "gentlemen do not read each other's mail." This kind of official policy continued until the 1941 attack on Pearl Harbor.

When Franklin Delano Roosevelt (FDR) took office in March 1933, things out of public view began to change. A good source of information on how he gained vital intelligence worldwide during the 1930's with the help of his friend and neighbor Vincent Astor is in Joseph E. Persico's book. *Roosevelt's Secret War*, Astor set up a special organization referred to as THE ROOM, which was located in a nondescript brownstone at 34 East 62nd Street in New York. Roosevelt, as Assistant Secretary of the Navy during the Wilson administration and later during his own presidency, worked on "War Plan Orange." It was a military plan of action if Japan ever attacked the United States. From his work on this, FDR became keenly aware of an area in the central Pacific referred to as the mandated islands; which included

4

the Carolines, the Marianas and the Marshall islands. Militarily, this knowledge went back to the 1840's from maps and reports from a whaling captain. Because this area surrounded our trade routes to the Philippines and China, Japan could block them at any time.

In 1920, the League of Nations had given Japan a mandate over these groups of islands. The natives were to be looked after and no military bases were to be built. Japan had taken control of this region in 1914 while Germany; owner of the islands was fighting World War I and considered the region part of their Empire. After complaints emerged in the League of Nations as to what Japan was doing in the central Pacific, the Japanese left the League and continued their plans.

During the 1920's, Major Pete Ellis of the Marines was sent into the mandated area to seek intelligence for the military. He had filed several reports before the Japanese poisoned him. The person sent to retrieve his body was also poisoned, basically losing his mind. Although our Government had submarines operating out of Pearl Harbor, only sea level observations could be made of the islands.

In the mid-1920's Colonel Billy Mitchell, a famous aviator who tried to persuade military leaders to believe in airpower, traveled in the central Pacific. He filed a secret report with the military that the Japanese were planning to attack the United States. The attack would be against Pearl Harbor and would likely take place on a Sunday morning. United States military leaders, however, felt that the attack would originate from bases in the mandated islands. It was thought that the Japanese were building a major naval base at Truck, an island in the Carolines. This began to be referred to as the Japanese Pearl Harbor or their Rock of Gibraltar. It had a tremendous harbor forty miles wide with only two heavily fortified entrances, and could hold most of the Japanese naval ships.

To offset what the Japanese were doing in the region, FDR directed the State Department to take control of three islands referred to as the "line islands." They were Jarvis, Howland and Baker, which were located south of the mandated islands. These islands had been abandoned by Great Britain for more than a year after that nation had finished mining guano, which was used as a fertilizer.

The documents concerning these takeovers are noted in Randal Brink's book, *Lost Star: The Search for Amelia Earhart*. He obtained them by using the Freedom of Information Act. The colonizers of these islands were primarily alumni from the Kamehameha School in Hawaii. Four men were sent to each island for three months. Although their primary job was operating the radios, could they have also been listening to more than just weather reports? If so, this would have concerned the Japanese. A fascinating story of life on these islands and a record of the three Japanese attacks on Howland Island in December 1941 can be found in E.H. Bryan, Jr.'s book *Panala'au Memoirs*.

The goal of the United States was to gather more intelligence on the mandated islands before Japan attacked. Neither Caucasians nor United States naval or civilian vessels were allowed to enter the mandated island region. Was anything planned for 1937 that might offer more intelligence about the region? As a member of the War Plan Orange committee, FDR had a possible answer to that question.

# 3 THE EARHART-ROOSEVELT RELATIONSHIP

Shortly after completing her first flight across the Atlantic Ocean in June 1928 with pilot Wilmer Stultz and co-pilot/mechanic Louis Gordon, Amelia received a telegram of congratulations from Franklin and Eleanor Roosevelt. They also invited Amelia to visit them in Albany or at their home in Hyde Park. At the time, he was the governor of New York.

That telegram was the beginning of a very close relationship between Amelia, her future husband George P. Putnam and the Roosevelt couple. There were many visits to Hyde Park and after Roosevelt became President, Amelia received invitations to dinners at the White House. She also received an open invitation to stay overnight at the White House, which she took advantage of when she was in the area.

On occasions when Eleanor was out of town and could not make a special lecture engagement, she would sometimes ask Amelia to speak in her place. Eleanor became so enthralled with Amelia's flight exploits that she wanted to learn to fly and set out to get a flying license. Franklin soon learned of that and stopped the plan immediately. In her autobiography, Eleanor wrote about Amelia, through the auspices of Eastern Airlines, taking her on her first night flight over Baltimore and Washington.

Amelia told her mother that she was going to campaign for FDR in the 1936 presidential election campaign. Since Amy was not a fan of the candidate, Amelia wrote to her mother the following in an undated and unsigned letter, "Please don't down the Roosevelt Administration – experiments carried out today point the way to a new social order when the government will be the voice of the proletariat far more than democracy ever can be." Because Amy was preparing for a trip to Europe, Amelia had been concerned that reporters might interview her mother and hear about her dislike for Roosevelt. Amelia wanted nothing to damage her relationship with the White House because she had future plans, which would require help from her good friends residing there.

On November 10, 1936, Amelia wrote a letter to FDR, a copy of which exists at the Franklin D. Roosevelt Library in Hyde Park.

Some time ago I told you and Mrs. Roosevelt about my confidential plans for a world flight. As perhaps you know, through the cooperation of Purdue University I now have a magnificent twin-motor all-metal monoplane especially equipped for long distance flying.

For some months Mr. Putnam and I have been preparing for a flight, which I hope to attempt probably in March. The route, compared with previous routes will be unique. It is east to west and approximates the equator.

Amelia continues giving FDR more detail about the route she is planning. Special survey work and map preparation is already underway. She mentioned Africa as being a less familiar portion of her route.

The chief problem is the jump westward from Honolulu. The distance hence to Tokio (Tokyo) is 3,900 miles. I want to reduce as much as possible the hazard of the take off at Honolulu with the excessive over-load. With that in mind, I am discussing with the Navy a possible refueling in the air over Midway Island. If this can be arranged I need to take much less gas from Honolulu and with the Midway refueling will have ample gasoline to reach Tokyo. As mine is a land plane, the seaplane facilities at Wake, Guam, etc. are useless.

This matter had been discussed in detail by Mr. Putnam and Admiral Cook, who were most interested and friendly. Subsequently, a detailed description of the project and request for this assistance was prepared. It is now on the desk of Admiral Standley, by whom it is being considered.

Some new seaplanes are being completed at San Diego for the Navy. They will be ferried in January or February to Honolulu. It is my desire to practice actual refueling operations in the air over San Diego with one of these planes. That plane subsequently from Honolulu would be available for the Midway operation. I gather from Admiral

Cook that technically there are no extraordinary difficulties. It is primarily a matter of policy and precedent.

Amelia goes on to tell FDR that the State Department is getting international permissions and has been very cooperative. The concluding paragraph in the letter is as follows:

Knowing your own enthusiasm for voyaging and your affectionate interest in Navy matters, I am asking you to help me secure Navy cooperation – that is if you think well of the project. If any information is wanted as to purpose, plans, equipment, etc., Mr. Putnam can meet anyone designated any time anywhere.

Randall Brink, an author and Amelia Earhart researcher, found a memorandum dated November 16, 1936 addressed to the Chief of Naval Operations which stated: "The attached letter was handed to me this morning, together with the information that the President hoped the Navy would do what they could to cooperate with Miss Amelia Earhart in her proposed flight and in this connection, contact should be made with her husband, Mr. Putnam."

Paul Bastedo, a member of the Navy Department, Office of Chief Operations, signed the memorandum. FDR moved quickly to notify the Navy and request their cooperation in helping his friend, thus honoring his friend's request.

In January 1937, Amelia sent a letter to FDR indicating that the difficult and costly maneuvers for refueling west of Hawaii had been obviated and instead she hoped to land on the tiny island of Howland. Immediately, FDR notified the navy to divert a shipment of materials being sent to another island in the region and deliver them to Howland Island. A request was also made to begin a landing strip on the island for Amelia.

An Assistant Secretary to the President wrote a letter to the President dated January 11, 1937, which included the following information: "An allocation of Federal funds has been made by the President to the Works Progress Administration to enable the Bureau of Air Commerce to carry out the construction of a field. I understand that the necessary equipment and labor for this work will be transported to Howland Island by the Coast Service on a boat scheduled to leave Honolulu on January 12, 1937." Amelia received a copy of this letter.

Since Roosevelt had been a member of the War Plan Orange before his presidency, he continued to serve during his Presidency. He was well aware of the lack of intelligence in the central Pacific.

FDR was one of the first persons to learn of Amelia's plans for a world flight as near to the equator as possible. The exact date when he began contemplating that Amelia might be able to assist in obtaining some additional intelligence as she flew across the Pacific is unknown. Could Amelia be persuaded to undertake a special secret mission for her friend, the President of the United States?

# 4 CRASH ENDS FIRST WORLD FLIGHT ATTEMPT

For her 39th birthday, Amelia received a Lockheed Model 10E Electra, named after the Lost Star of the Pleiades. Was this name foreshadowing Earhart's future?

The public was told that the plane was a gift from Purdue University where Earhart was a visiting professor teaching aviation to young women. She felt that women could be more than housewives. With the nation in the depths of the Great Depression, where did the university obtain the nearly $80,000 for the plane?

On page 76 in *Lost Star*, Randal Brink relates what Andrey A. Potter, Dean Emeritus of Purdue's Department of Engineering said about what really happened.

Miss Earhart's plane was purchased for her in the interest of national defense. The money was channeled through two private individuals to the Purdue Research Foundation. The monies, in the amount of $80,000 (equal to more than $1,000,000 in 1980 dollars) were then given to Miss Earhart so she could make the actual purchase of the aircraft. Among her tasks was the development of direction finding equipment for the U.S. Military.

Brink wrote further:

From several indications, including Earhart's own imprecise explanation, it can be inferred that the money was provided by a group of wealthy philanthropists. These include the two private individuals referred to in Dean Potter's statement Vincent Bendix, founder and chairman of the Bendix Corporation and J.K. Lily, the multimillionaire head of the J.K. Lilly conglomerate. Joining them was industrialist Floyd Odlum, owner of a vast cosmetics fortune, aviation enthusiast and fervent patriot. He was also married to Amelia's best friend, the accomplished pilot Jacqueline Cochran.

Another person who should be listed is Howard Hughes. In addition to being a close friend of Earhart and Cochran, he was also a business partner of Floyd Odlum. Hughes tried to keep his name and activities private. His associates stated that Hughes would be very unhappy to see his name in the press reports.

After Amelia received her new Lockheed, she made several flights with Paul Mantz to learn to fly the state of the art twin. An excellent pilot in his own right, he often worked in movies as a stunt pilot. He also had a relationship with Hughes, having helped him with his R-1 racing monoplane.

When announced in late 1936 that Earhart was to fly around the world, the Japanese became concerned. A flight close to the equator would come close to the southern border of the mandated islands. Would Amelia be encouraged to make a special flight over those islands to check on military installations in violation of the mandate by the League of Nations?

Japanese intelligence agents in California would have been assigned to investigate the capabilities of her Lockheed, the aerial cameras installed, the new infrared film, preparations for the flight and the persons visiting Amelia.

Japan needed a plan, one that they could deny ever happening. Thus, After Captain Kokichi Terada took command of the carrier *Akagi* on December 1, 1936; he received orders for a secret cruise to the Marshall Islands. This lengthy cruise presented an opportunity to evaluate the carrier, which had just undergone restoration at the Sasebo Naval Arsenal. Those orders had to have come from Yamamoto, the Commander of the Japanese navy, who would not have issued them without permission from Hirohito. If the United States government sent Amelia into the mandated islands as indicated by the information from California, the Japanese were going to ensure that she did not leave with any photographic evidence that could be used against them.

The carrier had to be on station in the southern part of the Marshall Islands before Amelia's departure from California on March 17, 1937. As it happened, that ship was seen in the Jaluit Atoll area with her destroyer escort prior to that.

On that date, back in Oakland, where it had been raining, it was late afternoon before a break in the weather allowed naval personnel to roll the Electra from the hangar. Paul Mantz, copilot of this flight performed the preflight inspection, including running up the engines. Amelia arrived at the airport in a naval staff car.

Also on board would be two navigators, Captain Harry Manning and Fred Noonan. Mantz was going on this first leg of the flight so he could meet his fiancé in Honolulu.

The Lockheed used only 1,897 feet for take off and soon was headed over the Golden Gate Bridge and on westward into clearing skies. The plane landed at Wheeler Field having set a new record for that trans-Pacific route of 15 hours and 47 minutes.

The following day Mantz ferried the Electra to Luke Field on Ford Island. To Joe Gervais, commenting later, the plane didn't look like the one that had landed at Wheeler Field the day before. He felt there were differences and that a second plane was involved in the flight.

On Monday, March 20th, Earhart, Noonan and Manning were ready to begin the flight to Howland Island. A small crowd had gathered at Luke Field to watch. Before the plane could reach take off speed, it swerved and began a ground loop with the landing gear folding under the fuselage. It came to a halt just off the runway.

Manning, who blamed Amelia for what happened, stated that there were sparks everywhere. If the plane had been loaded with more than 900 gallons of fuel, why wasn't there a fire? Was it the fact that Amelia had immediately shut down the engines? What surprised the first persons to arrive at the scene was that Noonan was collecting all his papers and seemed in no hurry to leave the plane. Hadn't he realized there was a chance of fire?

Within a few hours Amelia and her crew had boarded the Matson Line *S.S. Malolo*, which left Honolulu at noon. It would be interesting to know if reservations had been made prior to the crash. The plane would follow on a sister ship, the *S.S. Lurline*.

An Investigating Board convened at Luke Field on March 22nd. Amelia and her crew, however, had left within hours of the crash without discussing the accident with anyone. One might wonder if the crash had been an accident or something more. Had the fuel tanks, other than those necessary for takeoff been filled with water to prevent a fire? Had Amelia received last minute orders to abort the flight? Did Mantz instruct Amelia in how to do a ground loop? As a researcher, I have to ask these questions. "Secrets are kept secret by being passed on verbally and not put on paper for future generations to view."

When Earhart's wrecked plane arrived back in the United States, it was taken to the Pacific Airmotive Corporation (PAC). There, Amelia's friend Art Kennedy, an excellent mechanic who had assisted her with her 1935 record flight in a Lockheed Vega from Hawaii, had been assigned to work on the damaged plane. After 50 years of silence because of his promise to Amelia, he decided to tell the story of what really happed at Luke Field in his book *High Times*.

Before the Lockheed arrived at PAC, Kennedy was contacted by Eddie Cooper from the Bendix Corporation and told to carefully check the brakes, which Bendix had supplied. Cooper also shared some advance information concerning what happened at Luke Field. Kennedy wrote:

The bird arrived at PAC where we were to dissemble the wreck and disperse the parts for repair. At Amelia's request, I was put in charge of the crew. I soon got two surprises when we saw the condition of the plane as we began to lay it out on the floor.

The right wing and right gear had suffered all the damage, as was expected for a left ground loop, but the right gear was collapsed "outboard."

I asked Amelia, "What's going on here? This couldn't have been a normal ground loop. It was forced. Why?"

Very calmly she told me not to mention it and to mind my own business. So I told her that we better do something about the gear. She asked me why. I reminded her that the inspector was to arrive the next day to make an official accident report and that he'd know the gear and brake condition never would have been caused by an accident.

"Damn! I forgot about the gear," she said.

"Art, you and I are good friends. You didn't see a thing. We'll adjust the gear back over to make it look natural. Will you promise me never to say anything about what you know?"

I said, "Sure, Amelia." And I kept that promise for fifty years.

Later that night, Art, his wife and Amelia went out to dinner. Afterward, Amelia gave Art $50, which was half of a month's pay.

Before Amelia had arrived back in the United States, however, a new Lockheed Electra was being built for her. What was going on?

# 5    A SPECIAL PLANE FOR A SECRET MISSION

Before Amelia Earhart and her crew arrived back in the United States aboard the *S.S. Malolo,* a new plane for a second world flight was already being built at the Lockheed Aircraft facilities in Burbank, California. After the crash at Luke Field, Amelia and her husband had little to spend on a second effort. What entity had stepped forward to pay all her bills for a new plane and eventually the entire cost associated with the second world flight? For what reason had Earhart's dream of a world flight been commandeered?

Earhart's aide and secretary, Margo de Carrie who also handled her finances, told interviewers years later about the events that had occurred during that time period. First, Amelia had not received any bills for the second flight. Second, a number of very senior military officials visited the Putnam home in the Toluca Lake section of Hollywood.

During an interview in August 1980, Margo de Carrie told Randall Brink that "a significant turning point in the involvement of the military occurred after Earhart met with General Henry H. 'Hap' Arnold and General Oscar Westover, then the head of the U.S. Army Air Corps, at March Field Army Air Base. At one of these two meetings, or at some other point, officials were able to convince Amelia to accept a direct commission in the U.S. Military as a major, USAAF."

Brink continues in his book that

During her preparations, she was given permission to use the facilities at March Army Air Base, near Riverside, California. Normally, such military installations are strictly off limits to private activities. In fact, then, as now, laws and regulations prohibited the use of government property for the sole benefit of any individual. Finally, the financially strapped military could not afford to fuel its own military aircraft, much less provide fuel for Amelia Earhart. However, photographs show the Electra, surrounded by armed military police and being refueled at the base.

Margo de Carrie also told several interviewers that an emissary directly from the Oval Office came to the Toluca Lake house on three separate occasions. He was Bernard B. Baruch, FDR's dollar-a-year man, who had been an advisor to former presidents. He talked to Amelia about volunteering for an intelligence mission that would be assisted and underwritten by the military.

After Baruch's last visit, William T. Miller, a clandestine intelligence officer connected to top officials in Washington took up residence in the Putnam's home. His job would be to involve himself with the details of the plans for the second attempt. This information would be passed on to those in Washington with a need to know.

On page 8 of his book, *Amelia Earhart Survived*, Rollin C. Reineck listed the various government agencies and personnel who would facilitate the Earhart mission. He wrote that it "began at the highest echelon with the President of the United States." The following is a list of other involvement in the second flight.

      White House Staff
      United States Navy
      United States Coast Guard
      United States Army Air Force
      Works Progress Administration (WPA)
      Department of Commerce
        Eugene Vidal
        Robert Campbell
        William T. Miller
      Department of State
      Department of the Interior
        Richard B. Black
      Bureau of the Budget
      Department of Agriculture

"Strange indeed for one civilian, contemplating a stunt flight around the world to have involved almost the entire United States Government, up to and including the President. It is little wonder that the thought of a conspiracy entered into the Earhart Research."

Randall Brink reveals more about the plane that had been specifically built for Amelia. Previously, there had been nothing like it. When Paul Briand, asked Lockheed for a manual for the plane, he was told that no such manual exists. As you will see, her plane is a mixed bag of planes being put into one special plane which will go on to be known as the U-1. As opposed to the more recent U-2 spy planes which Lockheed also built for the C.IA.

Brink wrote,

The airplane Amelia flew around the world was a hybrid in many important ways. It had the size, outward appearance and higher gross weight of the Model 10, along with larger 550-horsepower Pratt and Whitney Wasp Senior engines; yet it was fitted with the more advanced constant-speed propellers of the Model 12. It also was capable of the Model 12's speed – as high as 240 miles per hour in level cruise flight. The plane was undoubtedly built using many Model 12 components, as R.T. Elliot has stated, and many others have suggested.

Mr. Elliott, an eleven-year veteran working at Lockheed Aircraft went on to tell Brink,

There was an Electra plane off the regular line. I recall that I was called off my regular duties several times to go to the experimental area. I was then directed to cut two 16-18 inch diameter holes to be used for the cameras (Fairchild aerial survey cameras, as documentation found later would show) which were to be mounted in the lower aft fuselage bay and would be electrically operated. There was a lot of modification required for this equipment. This was all done in the old Lockheed plant in Burbank, California. That bit about repairing her crashed Model 10 was just a ruse.

How could Amelia have taken reconnaissance photos of Japanese military installations at night? Woody Rogers sums up the answer in one word – infrared. During World War II, all photographs had to be taken during the day if conditions permitted. The laboratories of companies such as Eastman Kodak and Fairchild Camera began extensive and expensive experiments to develop the apparatus for using the new film. Much of the development had been completed in 1934, well in time for Amelia and Fred to use during the 1937 world flight.

Another device added to Amelia's flying laboratory included special photo flash bombs. In the *Nassau Daily News* there was an article about what had happened when the photo bombs were tested on Long Island.

Local residents who were terrified by explosions caused by Army maneuvers last night are wondering whether the bombing planes from Mitchell Field will be back on their practice flights again tonight.

Shortly after 6 o'clock last night two explosions caused by recently devised flares, which were used to enable the 18th Reconnaissance Squadron to photo at theoretical gun positions had residents swamping police and Army officials with telephone calls long after the maneuvers were over.

Captain Albert W. Stephens, who is a distinguished Stratosphere Flyer, developed the flares. They were released on parachutes and exploded shortly after so that time exposures could be made.

Colonel W. H. Frank, commanding officer at Mitchell Field, stated, "there was no danger in the flares, which dissolved after being set off."

There is no doubt that Amelia had the best intelligence gathering devices our military and private companies could provide. The information the world flyers could bring back would be priceless. Since the military was essentially devoid of intelligence from the mandated islands, much depended on what was recorded.

To continue the ruse, Amelia's new plane had her old number N16020. In Joe Klaas' book, *Amelia Earhart Lives*, there is a photo of the Earhart plane during the world flight with the new markings N16020. Joe Gervais, who had collaborated with Klaas on the book, once thought that there were at least five different airplanes involved in the world flight. I'm not going to further research this, as I believe there are more important matters to address.

Other events occurred after the modifications on Amelia's plane had been completed. Paul Mantz, her technical advisor, was replaced by Lockheed's Clarence L. "Kelly" Johnson. He would become famous for developing "state of the art" spy planes such as the SR-71; which had been developed in the 1950s for spying on the Russians during the cold war.

It was good, however, that Johnson was assigned to help Amelia learn the intricacies of her new plane, which was very technically advanced. It would take her time to get a feel for the extra weight and speed.

On September 27, 1957, Captain Paul L. Briand, Jr., who was considered the first Amelia Earhart researcher, received a letter from Johnson concerning his relationship with Earhart during this time. He wrote:

I knew Amelia Earhart very well and flew with her in making the basic test on the Electra. I had the highest regard for Amelia, not only as a fine person, but also as an excellent pilot. She was very careful, courteous and eager to learn. One outstanding fact about her, which always impressed me was that she would follow engineering recommendations exactly, contrary to my experience with a number of other women pilots, who would always ask me about problems they should have questioned the mechanics on and asked the mechanics problems in aerodynamics.

At the same time Amelia was getting acquainted with the new Electra, a Corporal Joseph Pelligrini was at Bolling Field, Washington, D.C being assigned to the Army Air Corps First Photo Mapping Group. He was participating in a very sensitive project. Corporal Joseph Pelligrini was drawing guidelines for cameras to be installed in a civilian aircraft.

By the time Gervais located the former photo corporal, he had been promoted to Lt. Col. Pelligrini and was very nervous talking with Gervais. He indicated that he had been in Hawaii during that time period. However, checking with military personnel, it was found that the Lt. Col. had indeed been assigned to Bolling Filed during 1937. Military personnel were still afraid to talk about the Amelia Earhart World Flight knowing that the story was "Top Secret" and a violation could end their military careers.

On May 22, 1937, Amelia Earhart with navigator Fred Noonan, her husband and mechanic Bo McNeeley left Oakland bound for Miami; the starting point for the second attempt. There was little publicity prior to this flight. It may have been a shakedown cruise with opportunities to land in the United States should the need arise. The entourage remained in Miami for several days while ostensibly; work was done on her radios. On June 1 at 6:00am, the Electra carrying Earhart and Noonan left Miami and headed toward Puerto Rico.

Unknown to the general public, she departed in the most sophisticated spy plane ever built. In *The Wild Blue Yonder*, Emile Gauvreau wrote, "Amelia Earhart left in an $80,000 flying laboratory capable of carrying sufficient gasoline for a nonstop flight of 4,000 miles, about 1,500 more miles than from Lae, New Guinea to Howland Island."

Thus, the world flight officially began with its scheduled stops, some shrouded in secrecy.

# 6 EAST TO LAE, GUINEA

On June 1, 1937 at 5:56 a.m., Electra NR16020 left Miami with Amelia Earhart as pilot and Fred Noonan as navigator. Immediately, she turned southeast toward Puerto Rico, their first stop on the world flight.

Several things should be noted. While Earhart and Noonan were in Miami, the *Daily Express*, an L-10E, a duplicate of Earhart's Lockheed but with 50 more gallons of fuel arrived in Miami from New York. Flown by pilots Dick Merrill and Jack Lambie, it had recently carried films of the Hindenburg's explosion and fire in New Jersey to London nonstop and returned in the same manner bearing films of the coronation of King George the VI.

There are continuing discussions among researches as to why that plane came to Miami while Earhart and Noonan were preparing for their world flight. It was reported at one point that Amelia and Fred disappeared for six hours and returned with a different plane. Was NR 16020 switched for NR 1059? More research is needed to ascertain what really happened in Miami. Obviously, what had been done was done secretly.

After landing in Puerto Rico, Amelia and Fred stayed overnight at the home of friend and pilot Clara Livingston. Of interest here is the fact that on May 16, 1936, George Putnam telegraphed Robert Gross, the President of Lockheed Aircraft directing him to proceed with building Amelia's Electra. For confidential reasons, however, he ordered Gross to name Livingston as the temporary purchaser until the plane was delivered to Amelia on July 24 with the assigned registration number of N16020. The bill of sale was not made public and the real meaning of this has never been explored. Was it an attempt to keep the public from asking too many questions too soon about a possible world flight?

It is not my intention to offer details for each of Earhart's stops during her flight. These are discussed in her book *Last Flight*, which contains excellent insight into each stop made and her reactions to the people and the local area. A few times Amelia was able to take some side trips, which were a pleasant relief from the rigors of flying. I will, however, highlight some events that were not mentioned in her book. Obviously, they were to remain secret.

Leaving Puerto Rico, they headed to South America and made several stops as they flew east to Natal. Leaving for Dakar, Senegal at 3:15 a.m. their cruising airspeed averaged about 150 miles per hour. Upon reaching Africa, Noonan told Amelia to turn south to Dakar. Thinking it was better to turn north, Amelia flew fifty miles that way and landed at Saint Louis, the headquarters of Air France. The following day she flew to Dakar. I wonder if there was more to this mistake than meets the eye. Suggested by researchers was that Amelia could have flown north of their published route across Africa from Dakar and taken photographs of Italian military installations. While 150 miles an hour was the announced speed of the Electra, in reality it could fly more than 200 miles an hour. This meant they could deviate from their published route, take the photographs and arrive at the original destinations without anyone knowing the difference.

Later, before leaving for a flight from Rangoon to Singapore, Amelia bet a KLM pilot twenty-five dollars that she could beat him to Singapore even though his Douglas DC-3 had a cruising speed of about 175 miles an hour. Earhart won the bet because she knew something the KLM pilot didn't. Her Electra was capable of speeds in excess of 150 miles an hour.

On June 21 she arrived at Bandoeng, Java in the Dutch East Indies. It was a large military base and a key one for KLM. The world flyers stayed for eight days. Pratt and Whitney sent new engines to Bandoeng for installation in NR 16020. How were they different from the ones she had is not known. It might be assumed that they were more powerful, which could help get the plane airborne from the three thousand feet of unpaved runway at Lae.

Why all the secrecy? Also involved was a flight to Surabaya and back. Was something being tested? Was there something secret that the public was not entitled to know?

A Bill Cole was listed as a Pratt and Whitney representative who had been in charge of bringing the engines to Bandoeng. Strangely, even though Cole was a pilot in World War II, his records have disappeared.

On June 29, Earhart and Noonan arrived at Darwin, Australia. Prior to their arrival, Lockheed had shipped another 10-E to another location. It is known, from people who were involved in the 10-E production at Lockheed that a plane similar to Amelia's had been built. Very probably, it had a mission in the world flight, but what part and where?

Earhart and Noonan arrived at Lae, New Guinea on June 30th after a flight of seven hours and forty-three minutes from Darwin. In Amelia's book is an account of her brief stay in Lae before taking off for Howland Island, 2,556 miles away. That part of the flight began one of the greatest mysteries in the history of our nation.

# 7   EARHART MISSION A FAILURE

In *Last Flight* Amelia wrote:

The landing field at Lae is one long strip cut out of the jungle, ending abruptly on a cliff at the water's edge. It is 3,000 feet long and firm under all conditions. There are hangars but a number of planes have to be hitched outside. I noticed all these planes were metal ones. In regular service here is another Electra, sister ship to my own.

When she states that there is a second Electra, a sister ship to her own at the airport, is she talking about the second Electra that was sent to Darwin, Australia by Lockheed? If so, why is it there at the airport in Lae?

In her book, she wrote about what she and Noonan did at Lae, but what is not mentioned is something that has become a mystery to researchers. Before leaving Lae, she is reported to have written a letter to her husband. The Putnam family has never made the letter public. Researchers Gervais and Klaas feel that it was a "Dear John" letter. Apparently the family felt the letter was too hurtful to be released. I have tried to obtain a copy of the letter. George Putnam's fourth wife Margaret refused requests to share it.

Prior to leaving on the world flight, Amelia spent more time with Jackie Cochran than her husband. Was this an indication of future events? What was Earhart's state of mind when she left Lae?

After taking off from Lae, Amelia headed toward Howland, but upon reaching 150 degrees east longitude, she turned 90 degrees to the north and headed toward Truk in the Japanese mandated islands. This deviation from her published route to Howland was part of a master plan to photograph the illegal Japanese military bases in the mandated island groups. Several parts of the plan have never been revealed. The Japanese had to believe that Amelia was still on her course to Howland, keeping basically south of the equator. To continue making the Japanese believe this, two or three Electras similar to Amelia's, with a man and woman crew were assigned to fly other paths near the equator.

Amelia pre-recorded radio messages that were broadcasted from several locations south of the equator, including Gardner Island. But, some transmissions, not the pre-recorded ones were heard by Pan American Airways (PAA) operators situated on Hawaii, Midway, Wake and Guam. After the flight, the Office of Naval Investigation (ONI) personnel ordered PAA personnel to destroy all these intercepts or be subject to imprisonment under the National Security Act. One set of these, however, was hidden and eventually given to Joe Gervais by Ellen Belotti, a secretary to the Director of Communications for the PAA.

After Earhart and Noonan had taken photographs of Japanese military installations, they were to deliver the film to the Navy at a secret location and then get lost. Ostensibly, this would allow naval personnel on ships and flying from carriers to search for the missing flyers and gain more information on the illegal bases. At that time, more than eighty percent of Americans, isolationist in their feelings, were opposed to more money being spent on military preparedness, but might be willing to spend money to find their heroine. This is what FDR hoped would be the case.

Of Course as soon as the Japanese learned of the world flight plans, the worry began since the route would be in the vicinity and within range of the mandated islands. If Amelia entered the mandated island area, she would not be allowed to leave.

As mentioned in Chapter 4, Japanese agents in the United States were monitoring flight preparations. Updated information on the Lockheed, the cameras, Amelia's military and governmental visitors would have been available. The Japanese surmised that a mission was being planned. They needed to be prepared and they were.

The carrier *Akagi*, with Captain Kochichi Terada aboard, was waiting in the Marshall Islands. To this day, the Japanese deny this occurred. The *Akagi* arrived in March 1937 for Amelia's first attempt and remained there. Apparently, the Japanese were expecting a second world flight to begin.

The most famous woman in the world was involved and much was at stake for Japan. It would be bad for their world image if it had become known what was planned if Earhart entered the mandated island area. Taking things a step further, if Amelia could be persuaded to come to Japan it would be a great step forward for that nation. Amelia spoke Japanese and had a tremendous knowledge of aviation, which could be helpful if Japan were forced to declare war on the United States. She also was a close friend of FDR, who had been adding to the Japanese hardships by stopping scrap iron and steel exports. Maybe Amelia could help in that area? No one knows the full extent of Yamamoto's or Hirohito's knowledge of what Amelia was to do. Did she, some may have wondered, want to change her lifestyle and escape from all the publicity?

While Earhart was in Bandoeng, Dutch East Indies, the U.S. State Department received the following report from one of its embassies: Captain Parker, a Norwegian subject, was captain of the *M.S. Fijian*, a motor ship, which sank after an explosion on March 25, 1937 near Jaluit in the Marshall Islands. Rescued by the Japanese, the captain and crew were eventually taken to Jaluit. Captain Parker stated that jaluit has an excellent harbor, which can only be entered by vessels under the guidance of pilots familiar with the reef formation in the channel. There were three Japanese naval destroyers and an aircraft carrier in Jaluit Harbor.

Although the carrier was not named, it can be assumed that it was the *Akagi*. All the other Japanese carriers were being prepared for an attack on China and were accounted for.

The U.S. Navy submarine, the *S.S. Argonaut* (SM-1) had been secretly penetrating the southern Marshall Island waters from its base in Hawaii. Certainly, the crew had to have observed the *Akagi* during one of its trips to the area and reported it to headquarters.

The following information is from *Stand By to Die* by Robert Myers who had been fifteen years old and had helped Amelia with flight preparations for both flights in Oakland. He had been listening to her flight on his father's shortwave radio after first hearing her voice when tuning the set. He reports the following:

Amelia was talking to Harry Balfour, the radio operator at Lae. She told Balfour that she is making her turn north at 150 degrees East Longitude. He replied that he knows nothing about any turn north. Irritated, she answered,

"They want me to fly directly north toward Truck. They should have told you."

Then she began talking about her husband. 'I know who is doing this to me. I knew I could not trust him. I don't know why he didn't tell me. I'll do it. But I won't do it for G.P., not for him. I'll do it for FDR!'

Amelia continued talking, 'There is more to this than what I told you. They knew this and didn't tell me anything. Maybe you are listening. Can you hear me?'

Does any of this have to do with the letter Earhart supposedly wrote her husband before leaving Lae? It is obvious that their relationship was not good.

Amelia and Fred overflew Truk, Ponape, Kwajelein, Wotje and Maloelap after encountering bad weather. Over Alingalapa, she had trouble even pronouncing the name. After stating that her windshield might break from the hail hitting it and taking the Electra to 12,000 feet, she reported the plane could not get above the storm. At times, Amelia indicated they were flying at about 250 miles an hour, a lot faster than the published 150.

When flying south after leaving Maloelap, Amelia suddenly cried out, "Oh my goodness! What is that? What are they trying to do? Why don't they go away and leave us alone!" She had spotted three Japanese fighter planes. One was above the Electra and the other two were flying on her right and left wingtips. Then their pilots began to fire machine gun bursts, continuing to try to force her down at Mili Atoll, where a Japanese base was located. Amelia cried out, "I won't do it."

Earlier she had radioed that she had seen three ships. "There is a fishing vessel, a small battleship and a large carrier. It's so huge. I have never seen a ship as big as this one."

Seeing an island ahead, she said, "We are going to land. The water looks smooth and calm in the lagoon." Then, "We hit east of the island."

Amelia reported that Fred was injured and bleeding. "We have a first aid kit. I'm all right, but Fred is not. He has a small cut on the left side of his forehead. I put a bandage on it."

After landing at Barre, Amelia radioed, "We're down. I told you where we were, but you didn't hear me. There is no one here! It is so hot. I can't stand it much longer. Why isn't anyone here?" At that time, she did not realize that she had landed on the wrong island.

She continued radioing that she had heard a message from the *S.S. Blackhawk*, a Navy supply ship en route from Guam to Manilla. There was no reply when Amelia called them. The ship, other than carrying cargo, had a secret role in the world flight.

During WWII, Bill Galten, a radio operator on the *Itasca*, was assigned to communicate with her. He told Rollin Reineck that he and his crewmates were on the *Itasca*, anchored just off shore of Howland Island and were waiting to guide the Electra to a landing. Later he concluded that Earhart had never intended to land there.

After learning that she never intended to land on Howland Island, only one thing came to mind. What was the right island? She was still more than 700 miles from Howland Island. There is definitely more to the story.

People other than Robert Myers, began to report hearing information about Earhart. Dorothy Kaucher, a teacher and writer from the San Jose State College in California landed on Wake Island August 15, 1937 as a passenger aboard the Pan American Clipper *Hawaii*. She was on a round trip from Oakland to Hong Kong. Having seen Amelia take off from Oakland on March 17th, she wanted to share in some of her experiences.

During her overnight stay at Wake, she talked about the Earhart flight with R.W. Hansen, a Pan American Airways radio operator there. Hansen stated,

> You know our radio got a signal from her plane 500 miles from here. It was a distress signal. I bet the Japs brought her down because she's seen too much. The way I dope it out is that she was on a high government mission, supported by the U.S. Navy, sent out to find out what she could about possible Japanese air bases, mainly if the Japs were fortifying the mandated islands like the Marshall Islands.

Years later, researcher and author T.D. "Buddy" Brennan met a Japanese veteran named Fuji Firmosa, who told him the following story:

When I was a young flight lieutenant, I was assigned to the aircraft carrier *Akagi*. We were on a training cruise near the Marshall Islands. Suddenly, we were called to battle stations and told that an American spy plane was attempting to photograph our installations. Shortly after, we were launched on a search mission. I soon saw an airplane with twin tails. To my surprise, I was told to force it down, fire on it if necessary. The pilot ignored me as I flew by, so I made a second run as a firing pass. I am not certain I hit it, but the plane went down and crashed just off one of the atolls. I learned later that it was Amelia Earhart. I could never learn more about the mission.

In an interview published in the *New York Times* on July 25, 1949, Amelia's mother Amy reported: "Amelia was on a secret mission for our government, which she could not reveal to me in 1937." Amy also stated that her daughter was permitted to broadcast to Washington; then she was taken to Japan. Who would have known enough about the Earhart story to tell Amy that her daughter was permitted to broadcast to Washington?

Shortly before he died in 1966, Admiral Chester W. Nimitz, Commander of the U.S. Pacific Fleet during WWII, told researcher Fred Goerner, "I want to tell you that Earhart and her navigator went down in the Marshall Islands and were picked up by the Japanese."

Admiral Edwin P. Layton was also appointed to the staff of Admiral Nimitz as Chief of Intelligence. Layton, who spoke fluent Japanese, had been assigned earlier to Ambassador Joseph Grew's staff in Japan (1932 through 1941) and was well informed about the Earhart incident and the Japanese rescue.

Cardinal Spellman, also a close friend of Admiral Nimitz and FDR, had a large role in the Earhart story and shared his information with Nimitz.

It is important to know that FDR invoked a secret Executive Order that the Earhart incident was considered Top Secret. Anyone releasing information regarding what they knew had happened on

July 2, 1937 and afterward, was in serious trouble and could find themselves without any retirement plan or worse. FDR had an election to win in 1940 and could not allow the American people to know the truth. Additionally, to this day, the Amelia Earhart incident is still considered a matter of national security. Some Earhart researchers have discovered this the hard way.

Thus, we leave Earhart down near Barre Island having difficulty enduring the intense heat and humidity. Noonan has a head wound and an injury to his knee, which had become infected. The natives, afraid to come forward and offer assistance in fear for their lives, remained in the jungle and watched the arriving Japanese.

# 8   EARHART AND NOONAN RESCUED

Amelia later radioed, "The Japanese naval personnel arrived in a shore boat and they are beating Fred."

On July 3 at 1300 hours, the battleship *USS Colorado* under the command of Captain Wilhelm L. Friedell left Hawaii for Howland Island. The ship had been on a month-long naval ROTC cruise with 200 cadets from the University of California at Berkeley aboard. Also there were guests from other universities onboard.

Before leaving Hawaii, Friedell had conferred with Rear Admiral Orin Murfin, Commandant of the Fourteenth Naval District at Pearl Harbor and Commander Kenneth Whiting, who was the Commanding Officer of the Fleet Air Base. With other officers at the base, they devised a potential search plan to find the Electra. Had Friedell been given information on the Master Plan, which called on him to reconnoiter Japanese military bases while supposedly searching for the Electra?

On July 5, the *Colorado* approached the *Itasca*. After refueling and replenishing the ship's stores, the battleship left for the area to initiate the planned search. Did Friedell know that naval personnel were monitoring Japanese radio transmissions and had real time information as to what was happening to Earhart on Barre Island?

The aircraft carrier *USS Lexington*, with sixty planes aboard, along with three destroyers departed Pearl Harbor for Howland Island on July 8th. Several of the civilians on the ship kept personal diaries. Information concerning the search for Amelia and her Electra is provided in the book *The Hunt for Amelia Earhart*.

Although the mission was secret and only those with a bona fide need to know had been informed of the big picture. The commanders of the *Colorado* and *Lexington* had to know what was happening to undertake their mission.

During a Congressional Hearing in Washington, it was stated that much of the intelligence gathered on the Japanese mandated islands was obtained during the search for the missing flyers. Thus, at least part of the world flight mission was a success.

In 1937, the United States was woefully unprepared for war with Japan. The Empire of the Rising Sun has several military assets near Barre Island, including the *Akagi* with its complement of eighty aircrafts as well as a battleship and several other support ships.

Yes, the United States had the submarine *USS Argonaut* in the area, but there was little its crew could do. The water on the lagoon side of Barre Island where the Electra was located was too shallow to attempt a rescue. Because of the Japanese military presence so close to the island no one could interfere with the rescue of Amelia, Fred and protect the Electra.

After the Japanese were certain the Americans would not attempt a rescue, they initiated Phase Two of their plan. The *Akagi* and its support ships began their surveillance work checking out the United States, British and Australian installations. Although the U.S. Navy realized what was happening, there was not an effective way, short of a war to stop it.

Four million dollars was spent on the search for Amelia Earhart, even though FDR had to have known from his intelligence sources that there was little he could do. He also knew that if the isolationists and conservative antagonists in Congress found out what Roosevelt was truly up to, he'd be in serious trouble.

Klaas emailed Reineck, "Why couldn't the Navy go ahead and conduct a survey without making such a 'cloak and dagger' operation out of it?" The answer includes both national and international politics. America's military had been weakened by the Great Depression and money to improve it was scant. The anti-war isolationist lobby in Washington was powerful and would oppose any expenditure for such a survey. But, if it could be hidden behind a search for Earhart, even the isolationists might support it.

FDR and those who planned the Earhart mission were fooled into thinking the Japanese would take no action against a famous woman pilot who had taken photographs of their military installations. How naïve the President and his planners were!

On July 16th the official search ended. Five years later, Charles Palmer wrote an interesting article titled *Was Amelia Earhart the War's First Casualty?* This appeared in the November 1942 issue of *Skyways* magazine. He wrote that the rendezvous point for the *Lexington* on its return voyage to Hawaii was 5.50 North Latitude and 17.2:15 East Longitude; a location a few miles southeast of Knox Island and adjacent to Mili Atoll. Was this the island where Amelia was supposed to have landed all along? Instead, she was forced to come down on Barre Island.

The Japanese notified the United States government that none of their ships were in the area. That was a lie since fighters from the *Akagi* had forced Amelia down. They were, however, sending *Koshu*, a survey ship to look for the Electra. What they did not reveal was that they already knew where she was and planned to pick up the flyers and the airplane. Under the command of Hanijiro Takagi, that ship was able to navigate the shallow waters in the lagoon near Barre Islands. Thus, the Electra could be loaded on a barge and towed to the ship.

Vincent Loomis reported in *Amelia Earhart, the Final Story*, that

On July 2, 1937, the *Koshu* was anchored at Ponape (in the Caroline Islands), where it received orders to proceed to the Marshall Islands and 'search' for Amelia Earhart. By July 9th, it was on its way. Only the *Koshu*, capable of retrieving small floatplanes, took part in what the Japanese promised was a search, but its log entries revealed no search effort. With a specific mission to perform it went straight to Jaluit and anchored there on July 13th to load coal.

One of those loading coal was Tomaki Mayazo, who heard the crew members of the *Koshu* excitedly mention that they were on the way to pick up two American flyers and their aircraft, which had crashed at Mili. After picking up Amelia, Fred and the Electra, the *Koshu* returned to Jaluit. On July 19th the Japanese Government officially gave up its search for Earhart.

In later years, several Earhart researchers interviewed Bilimon Amran, a local businessman. People said he was honest and could be trusted. Consistently, he had told the same story.

During July 1937, I was residing in Jaluit, the site of a major Japanese naval base. I was working as a medical corpsman at the naval hospital. Midmorning one day, a Japanese Navy ship came into the harbor and the Chief

34

Medical Doctor brought me onboard. The uniformed crew and officers were present. Sitting in a deck chair was an American woman. Nearby was a thin American man, who appeared to be injured, sitting on a hatch cover. The Japanese doctor had me tend to the man's wounds, which were not serious. I recall he had a cut over his eye and deep gash above his knee. I tied the knee wound with a paraply (compress with iodine).

The lady looked to be in good health and needed no treatment. These two Americans did not seem to be held as prisoners at the time. But, the Japanese crew was in awe of the woman, because she was a pilot, a rarity anywhere then. I didn't speak English, so I could not talk to the Americans. A Japanese officer told me that the Americans had flown their plane from New Guinea trying to reach Howland Island. They became lost and tried to make it back to Gilberts, crashing near Mili Atoll. The Japanese found them and rescued them. The same Japanese officer took me to the rear of the ship and showed me their airplane, which was suspended in a sling. They had used their crane to hoist it.

It was definitely a modern American plane; shiny silver with two engines and the left wing was broken. The crew referred to the lady as 'Meel-ya.' She wore a white blouse with a kerchief around her neck. The American man had blue eyes and a thin mustache. Both looked very tired, but in good health. The Japanese officer mentioned that they would probably be transferred to Saipan. I never saw them again.

It was interesting that the Japanese officer told Bilimon that the Americans were lost and had crashed. There was no mention that they had been on a spy mission and forced down. Did the officer know? If so, he was not revealing anything.

While doing research in Japan, Loomis' assistant Tatsu Ehara collected an initial batch of records from government sources. These contained the message traffic between Japan and its outposts and diplomatic offices from July through December 1937. In them he found information that the Japanese had been watching Earhart's flight as it progressed around the world and then into sensitive areas in the mandated islands. There was much confusion in Japan about diplomatic messages.

When the Electra was reported missing in the World Press, messages among Japanese government agencies began to reflect panic over the consequences. Subordinates were not able to make decisions about what to tell the U.S. Government and George Putnam as they sought permission to enter the Marshall Islands and look for the lost Electra. Dispatches reflected Japanese orders to keep the search efforts away from the islands. There were grave concerns about how best to mask the situation since an entire Japanese Navy Task Force was supposed to be prowling the seas on behalf of the Americans.

Finally, Yamamoto took the matter into his own hands and sent messages to aid Japanese diplomats in responding to pressures from the West to be let into the mandates. Clearly implied in his statements was that under no circumstances would the Americans be allowed to search for Earhart.

But what was happening on Barre Island during the several days after Amelia arrived? How did the pair protect themselves from the elements? Dealing with tremendous heat and humidity along with daily rainstorms had to have taken its toll. Also, one has to wonder what was going through Amelia's mind as they waited, not knowing what was going to happen.

In 1987, the 50th anniversary of Amelia's flight, the Marshall Island Postal Service released a block of four stamps, one of which portrayed two natives at the jungle's edge looking at the stranded Electra. During Loomis' visit to the Marshall Islands, this is what Jororo and Lijon; the two natives reported.

Sometime before the war they had seen an airplane land on the reef about 200 feet offshore. They said they were frightened and hid in the jungle. They remained hidden while what they thought were two men get out of the plane into a yellow raft and come ashore. Shortly after they got on the island a fisherman saw them bury a silver container. In a short while the Japanese arrived and started to question the two flyers, one of who was taller than the other.

During the questioning, the Japanese started to slap the fliers, at which time one of them started to scream. At that point the two natives realized one was a woman. They stayed hidden because they knew the Japanese would have killed them for what they witnessed.

The stamps, first day covers and people interviewed who had seen what happened in the overall landing and rescue is consistent with what is portrayed and stories that they tell. Therefore, there should be no dispute as to what really occurred.

In an email to a friend and fellow researcher, Joe Klaas summarized the big picture as to what he felt had happened.

Amelia Earhart wasn't some unknown Frenchman cruising on a yacht. She was the most famous woman in the world, on postage stamps of several countries. The Japanese could have scored one of the biggest public relations good will victories in history by announcing they had rescued this darling of the world. If they treated people as spies, they had no reason to believe they were spying. And knowing she was not a spy would have made it easy for Franklin Roosevelt to reveal that she was a prisoner and ask for her release, unless she had been caught red-handed spying for him. How else can the diplomatic silence and secrecy of two major powers like the United States and Japan be explained other than that the most popular woman on earth had both been caught spying and had been involved in a secret illegal operation by the White House, which endangered the life of America's flying sweetheart. The public relations cost to both nations would be unbearable. It was America's darkest secret, which was finally revealed in World War II.

Word circulated among the Marshallese that the *Kushu* left Jaluit and took the Americans to Roi-Namur, a major Japanese air base in the Marshalls. From there the two were flown to Saipan in a twin-tailed amphibious aircraft, probably a Type 91 HiroH4HI. Later, the Electra, having been stored on Emidj Island, just north of Jaluit, was taken to an island in the eastern chain of the Marshalls where it remains today. Before the end of WWII, the Japanese had buried it along with several other aircrafts.

As Bilimon Amran had said after seeing the Americans on the *Koshu*, he did not think they were prisoners. From all the documents I have read, I agree with him.

Both Hirohito and Yamamoto were controlling Amelia's well-being. That was very important to both men. Earhart's future cooperation would be of extreme importance to Japan's desire for world dominance. They needed her to be on their side to aid in both building and flying various types of airplanes. Also, she had worldwide contacts and closely tied to Roosevelt, a proverbial thorn in the side of the Japanese.

Several researchers, who have written books in recent times, believe that Saipan was the last stop and that Earhart and Noonan were executed there. To promote such an idea is to state publicly that the Japanese were not capable of analytical thinking at the time. Several top Japanese officials who were on Saipan have indicated that neither Amelia nor Noonan were executed there.

In the next chapter, information will be presented from the Earhart file located in the U.S. State Department's archives. On those pages is more data about the Earhart mission and its ramifications.

# 9 EARHART AND JAPANESE-SAIPAN NEGOTIATIONS

Winston Churchill said, "Courage is what it takes to stand up and speak; courage is also what it takes to sit down and listen." Amelia Earhart could only listen as the Japanese formulated what they were going to do with her. Officials stationed on Saipan were not the ones determining it. Top officials were arriving from Japan to meet with her. Quite likely they were representatives of Admiral Isoruko Yamamato. The Emperor of Japan would also be kept informed as to how the negotiations were proceeding.

According to the Japanese Government, Earhart was not considered a prisoner on Saipan as some researchers and several Saipanese residents alleged. Note that the Government's allegation wasn't that she was on Saipan, but whether she was imprisoned on Saipan.

Joe Gervais and Fred Goerner stated that eyewitness accounts from Saipan residents indicated that Earhart was quartered in a hotel, not a prison – consequently, making the Japanese statement true.

Commander Paul Bridwell, Naval Commandant of Saipan in 1962 stated,

The testimony of the Saipanese people cannot be refuted. A white man and a white woman were undoubtedly brought to Saipan before the war. Quite probably they were Earhart and Noonan. The Japanese brought them there from the Marshall Islands.

Bridwell goes on to state:

A Japanese supply vessel was used to take them from Jaluit Atoll to Yap in the Carolines...and a Japanese seaplane flew them to Saipan. That's why the Saipanese interviewed said they came from the sky.

The Commander went on to say,

I think you'll find all the proof you need contained in radio logs of four U.S. logistics vessels, which were supplying the Far East Fleet in 1937. Remember the *Gold*

*Star, Blackhawk, Chaumont* (later named the *Ogala*) and the *Henderson*. They intercepted certain coded Japanese messages that I think you'll find fascinating reading.

Vincent Loomis obtained the above information during an interview. As I tried to follow up, a problem occurred. All the radio logs Commander Bridwell talked about during his interview had disappeared. Apparently, the U.S. Navy and the Government did not want researchers reading those logs.

Before the Japanese took Amelia into custody, she heard a message from the *Blackhawk* and tried to respond to it without success. Radio operators on the *Blackhawk* had to have been tuned into Earhart's radio messages as she flew through the mandated islands on her mission. These messages were kept secret and unavailable to researchers or the general public.

It can be assumed that the radio operators on the *Blackhawk* and most probably, the three other supply ships were listening in on Japanese transmission concerning Earhart's being forced down in the Marshall Islands as well all the confusion as to what to do with the flyers. This meant that the United States government knew in real time what the Japanese were planning to do with them.

As reported by some of the Saipanese interviewers, Amelia was quartered in a Garapan City hotel controlled by the military, the *Kobayoshi Royakan*. She was seen on a number of occasions walking around the area. A young girl named Matilde San Nicholas, who lived next door to the hotel, remembered that Earhart would stop by and help her with her geography and even gave her a ring. This was, most probably the pearl ring given to Amelia just before she left Lae. In the group photo taken there, the woman believed to be the wife of Tom O'Dea, the President of Guinea Airways, Ltd., is holding it prior to giving it to Amelia.

During this time period, one might wonder what Amelia was thinking and feeling. Was she wondering what the Japanese planned to do with her or did she already know? There are reports that she was seen with high-ranking Japanese officials who had come to Saipan to meet with her. One report from a group of Saipanese indicated they watched Amelia get out of a car with a Japanese admiral and enter military headquarters. She was reported to have been wearing a pink print dress and carrying a handbag.

To verify this, a report from the Gervais files stated the following:

One morning Louis Igatol, reporting to work at the Tanapag Harbor Seaplane Base, saw the Admiral's car pull up in front of the main office. The driver opened the door and he saw Amelia get out of the car with the Admiral. She was wearing a light blue jacket, blue pants and carrying a sling purse over her shoulder. He never saw this admiral again and thinks he came from Japan or some other island, Honcho-Kobito!

With several top researchers concluding Amelia and Noonan had been executed, it would be easy to convince others. Amelia Earhart was the most famous woman flyer in the world. Just her knowledge of aviation alone would justify the Japanese wanting her safely in Japan and being used in their military. The Japanese were interested in expanding their Empire, not putting a supposed spy to death. As a result of Earhart's failed mission, no damage was done to the Japanese military intelligence nor was anything of importance compromised and given to the United States. The films were never delivered to the U.S. Navy. While one has to wonder, was there any contact between Earhart and the Japanese before she left on her world flight? She may have not been happy and was possibly looking for a change in her life.

The Japanese knew that Amelia had worked closely with Clarence "Kelly" Johnson, a top design engineer for Lockheed in the development of her spy plane, the most advanced of its time. She was also involved with her close friend Howard Hughes and his H-1 racing plane, probably the fastest plane in the world. The Japanese needed a new fighter after witnessing their experiences in invading China. Yamamoto knew this and was an advocate of air power, particularly for his carriers. He fought those in Japan who supported battleships, almost losing his life to an assassin.

Could Amelia's influence with Roosevelt be used to help the Japanese obtain some concessions such as making sure the stream of raw materials imported from the United States continued?

Yamamoto was also very concerned about the safety of his good friend Hirohito when the war began with the United States. Maybe Amelia could help secure the safety of the Emperor and his family when the war began? The answer was yes and the admiral put this into effect soon after Amelia's arrival in Japan.

Taking all the aforementioned events into consideration, can anyone believe that Yamamoto or the Emperor would allow Amelia or Fred to be executed on Saipan? She was a valuable asset to Japan's future and was to be protected.

Researchers have conducted hundreds of interviews. Joe Gervais and his partner Lt. Col. Robert S. Dinger did some of the best. Unfortunately, the original documents submitted at the military hearing were never returned. The Japanese were not going to let the Saipanese know what their plans were for Amelia and Fred. In fact, deception was used to mislead them.

Decoy planes had been used by the United States as part of the Earhart Mission Master Plan. Had one or more of these Electras, crewed by a man and a woman, and arrived at Saipan in 1937? Had any of these crews been imprisoned and eventually executed on Saipan? It is known that a Japanese-American woman was publicly executed on Saipan. Were the residents led to believe that this person was, in fact, Earhart or one of the other woman crewmembers?

Amelia had known Yamamoto personally, having taught him English when he was a student at Harvard University from 1919 to 1921. He would become her mentor from the time of her arrival in Japan until he was shot down in April 1943. Some of his staff had become overly concerned about their relationship. Even so, her having known him at Harvard must have helped her in making the transition to a new life.

Much information was presented during a conference of the Amelia Earhart Society in August 1993 at the Flying Lady in Morgan Hill, California. That was the last big conference attended by most of the Earhart researchers. A lot of the information shared during this meeting will be referred to during the remaining chapters of this book. Where did much of this information presented come from? It had come from the highest government files, supposedly unavailable and to that of a new researcher who found something of interest and recorded it.

In February 1993, a "high level government official" from the State Department, who had seen the Earhart file, called a well-known researcher and said,

It's time for the public to know the truth. Amelia Earhart was captured in the Marshall Islands by the Japanese and taken to Saipan and later to Japan. As she was going to Japan by ship, she was ravished by some of the Japanese escorting her. Rumor says that Yamamoto was so infuriated at the way she was treated while being transported, that he had those responsible immediately executed.

To date, the State Department has refused to make information on Earhart public. The only logical reason that can be given for this secrecy is that we are afraid to offend Japan. But, consider the American people who would like to know what happened to their heroine. Don't they have a right to know the truth? They have been told for 78 years that Amelia and Fred died somewhere in the Central Pacific.

With information provided by the State Department in 1993, the story of the flyer's executions on Saipan needs to be stopped and exchanged for the truth. The Japanese certainly didn't want the people there to know that Earhart was being transferred to Japan. Along with the deceptions from the Japanese, Earhart researchers had to be given misleading information also.

This author believes that Fred Noonan remained on Saipan until American forces invaded it in 1944. He then returned to the U.S. as part of the witness protection program. After being recognized in California by someone who had known him in 1937, he told that person that if he ever said anything to anyone, he would personally kill him. Another occasion of Noonan being recognized occurred in mechanic Art Kennedy's shop. One day Noonan walked in, identified himself, visited for several hours and then left.

Regarding Amelia's new life in Japan, not much hard information exists as to what occurred during those years. However, in the next chapter I will discuss what I was able to find on her life in Japan.

# 10 AMELIA EARHART BEGINS HER NEW LIFE IN JAPAN

Franklin Roosevelt once said, "We have always held to the hope, the belief, the conviction that there is a better life, a better world beyond the horizon."

Is a better world what Amelia Earhart was hoping for as she traveled from Saipan, bringing her closer to her new home? Had Admiral Yamamoto's representatives informed her of what to expect in Japan during their meetings in Saipan? Amelia was not a prisoner, but a very important person to the Japanese cause. Her welfare was of great concern to Yamamoto and the Emperor of Japan.

Amelia's time on the ship had not been uneventful. As mentioned in Chapter 9, she had been ravished by some of her Japanese escorts during the voyage to Japan. Yamamoto took appropriate action to let the people of Japan know that Amelia Earhart was his friend and nothing harmful was going to happen to her while he was alive. When the Emperor learned what had happened on the ship, he too was outraged. He was soon to have a very close relationship with Amelia. How could he make things up to her?

Since code breakers in the United States had broken the Japanese diplomatic code, Joseph Grew, the ambassador to Japan should have known when Amelia would arrive. Had he or any of his representatives tried to contact the famous flyer after the ship had docked? Since FDR had issued a secret Executive Presidential Order that the Amelia Earhart mission was Top Secret, Grew could write nothing about Amelia in his autobiography. He had been in Japan since 1932 and on December 8, 1941, he was interned by the Japanese and released with a number of others in August 1942. Thus, since he and Earhart had both been in Japan at the same time, there may well have been some meeting between them. This is, of course speculation on this author's part. Several FBI reports contain information that the Japanese people knew Earhart was in Japan.

Also contained in the State Department file is that soon after arriving in Japan, Earhart had an operation. It isn't known what the operation was for, but information surfaced that the operation was not successful and ended up with the mutilation of her "lower parts." How had this information been transmitted to the United States? Certainly lines of communication existed between the United States and Japan as to what was happening to Earhart.

After she had left Saipan for Japan, there was a report from Garapan that a large quantity of blood was found in Amelia's bed at the military-run hotel. Was this real or a plant to give the Saipanese the feeling that Earhart was sick or had possibly died – all this to cover her transfer to Japan. If it was authentic, did it have anything to do with the operation performed after she had arrived in Japan? The fact that the "lower parts" of her body were badly scarred remains important information to recall at a later time.

After the ordeal during her voyage to Japan and the operation, time was needed for recovery. Her being able to speak some Japanese was probably helpful. Reports indicated that she was placed in an apartment in the Imperial Palace, where personnel would have the best of everything to assist her in recovering.

Something else was in motion here with Earhart being moved into the Imperial Palace. Yamamoto knew that Japan was eventually going to attack the United States and was concerned about Hirohito's safety. By putting Amelia in the Imperial Palace and informing the United States, an agreement was reached that the United States would not bomb the Imperial Palace if the Japanese took care of Amelia.

Edwin P. Hoyt's book *Yamamoto, The Man Who Planned the Attack on Pearl Harbor*, contains information about the kind of person the Admiral was. Born in 1884, Isoruku was thirteen years older than Amelia. The youngest of three children, he obtained much of his early education from Christian missionaries. Though he never became a Christian, he had a bible, which he often read. That experience gave him exposure to both the English language and American customs. After those years, he attended the new Imperial Japanese Naval Academy where he did very well because advancement was based on ability and not politics.

Yamamoto was an honorable and ancient name in Japanese history. It was not, however, his birth name. For several years the Yamamoto clan had been searching for a new leader and Isoruko's performance at the academy had been so impressive that they asked him to take the family name and responsibility. The change was duly recorded in the Yamamoto clan records. Thus, in 1916, he became Lieutenant Commander Isoruko Yamamoto in the Imperial Japanese Navy.

In August 1939, Japan notified the State Department that Mrs. George P. Putnam had renounced her U.S. citizenship. "Mrs. Putnam wishes the U.S. Government to henceforth consider her a national of the Nipponese Imperial Islands."

Could there have been another reason? If Earhart were to become an important part of the Japanese military forces, including becoming the Air Commander, military personnel would more readily accept a Japanese citizen.

George Palmer Putnam divorced Amelia in 1939, far sooner than normal for a person who was only declared missing. Had he known that his wife would not be returning any time soon? With the letter he received from her before leaving Lae, he must have reasoned that there was little chance for reconciliation.

Yamamoto was involved in Amelia's well being in Japan from 1937 through April 18, 1943, at which time he was shot down during an inspection trip while a passenger in a Mitsubishi G4M. As the plane was approaching Balalae Airfield in the Solomon Islands, two pilots in P-38s attacked and killed the Admiral. After Yamamoto's death, it appeared that the Emperor became her mentor. Representatives of the Vatican, including Cardinal Spellman, made periodic visits to Japan to ensure the agreement was enforced. Additionally, he was looking after the more than 100,000 Catholics who were living there.

In *Amelia Earhart Lives*, which Joe Klass wrote using Joe Gervais' research, the following appeared:

It is our opinion that in 1937, an American spy was intercepted and captured in the Pacific by the Japanese, who tried to use her to blackmail the United States into signing a Consular Treaty favorable to Japan. Her name was Amelia Earhart. The Japanese gave her the code name "Tokyo Rose." President Roosevelt refused to be blackmailed, refused to admit to American espionage by demanding her return and left her to the fate traditionally reserved for spies who are caught. Amelia was totally abandoned by her country and her good friend Franklin Roosevelt.

The Japanese, who could not admit they had caught Earhart spying without disclosing flagrant violations of international law in secretly constructing bases in the mandated islands, allowed her to survive in anonymity for a very important reason.

Yes, Amelia was alone in Japan. Roosevelt was protecting himself, so much for friendships if they caused problems. He had the 1940 election to worry about.

Amelia needed time to recover and adjust to her new life in Japan. The Japanese needed her in good health for all that was to follow. She would be needed to help solve a major military problem. Their naval pilots had performed poorly during the July 7, 1937 attack on China. Pilots of British and French planes took a severe toll on the Japanese planes. If the Japanese were going to continue their quest to secure Asia and someday attack the United States, a fighter that could dominate all others was necessary.

The Japanese knew about a plane they would like to copy and felt that Earhart could help them get the drawings. Japanese representatives had spent a great deal of time in the United States checking all the military assets. Amelia's friend owned the airplane they were interested in. Certainly, that individual had to have been concerned about her safety in Japan. Perhaps a deal could be made.

First Day Covers released from the Marshall Islands Post Office depicting Amelia Earhart's world flight and crash into the Marshall Islands.

Amelia Earhart

First Day of Issue

Colorano "Silk" Cachet

Amelia Earhart

First Day of Issue

Colorano "Silk" Cachet

50

# MARSHALL ISLANDS

CAPEX '87

Official First Day of Issue

# MARSHALL ISLANDS

CAPEX '87

Official First Day of Issue

# INTERIM

Leading into the next chapters, I ask you, the reader to keep an open mind. When Amelia indicated to me that she wanted me to tell her story, she did not tell me to "include this or that event or don't include anything that would reflect poorly on me." From the beginning of my research, I have been looking for the truth.

During the eight years in Japan, Amelia was involved in activities she was not pleased with or proud of. The first four years while she was in Japan, the United States and Japan were not at war. Was she a double agent for Roosevelt?

Toward the end of the war a flow of intelligence was coming to the Office of Strategic Command (OSS) via the Vatican. It seems that an entity was there in contact with Earhart on a regular basis. After the war, some German nuns referred to Amelia as Cardinal Spellman's girlfriend who was living in the Imperial Palace. They wanted to make sure that the United States troops got her out.

The Vatican closed their Archives in 1937. We don't know the exact reason why this was done. Spellman, however, was a representative of the Pope, who sent him on several assignments before and during the war.

At the end of the war, General MacArthur, while still in the Philippines was briefed on the Earhart situation by Jackie Cochran and Cardinal Spellman. Possibly, at that time, the decision was made not to force the Emperor to stand trial. MacArthur thus realized that at a trial of the Emperor the details concerning Amelia's life in Japan could be embarrassing for the United States.

After the war, MacArthur and Amelia became friends. Would that happen if he felt she was a traitor? Also, MacArthur might have learned that she had been the Air Commander of the Japanese Air Force.

I will explain what I know about Amelia's activities in Japan in the upcoming chapters. Readers can decide what to believe. She was never a prisoner of the Japanese after her capture in 1937.

However, what type of controls did they have over her during those years in Japan?

# 12 THE JAPANESE ZERO A6M

In early 1937 the Imperial Japanese Navy (IJN) began looking for a new fighter aircraft. In May, specifications were sent to Nakajima and Mitsubishi. Both firms started preliminary design work. Soon, however, Nakajima dropped out, finding the specifications too demanding.

At Curtiss Aircraft, located in Garden City, Long Island, Hiro Horikoshi, a designer for Mitsubishi had worked as an inspector on the P-6s built there and exported to Japan. He knew and had talked with Amelia Earhart on several occasions in the early to mid-1930's. During the spring of 1938, they were together in Japan when the early wind tunnel test on the Zero was done. In July 1939, she first flew the Type 00 carrier deck fighter at the Gifu Air Base in Kakamigahara. Also of interest is a photo in the State Department file of her standing by a twin-engine "Randy," which was never put into production. Joe Gervais received the above information from Mr. A.D. Gibson who had access to Earhart's State Department file.

In 1973, Bob Wilson, a Vice President of Texas Instruments visited Gervais in Las Vegas and mentioned that during a Japanese Manufacturing Quality Control tour of the plant, Hiro Horikoshi, former Zero designer had led the group. During a discussion about World War II at the luncheon, he mentioned that the greatest Japanese Air Marshall was a woman. The Japanese would not mention Amelia Earhart's name but this would be the closest they would come to making a statement about her.

The date when Earhart became the Air Commander is not known. Her office was in the Dai Ichi Military Building near the Imperial Palace. This will be discussed later on.

The Japanese were skillful at copying military equipment from other countries. Did an airplane exist that met the specifications that Mitsubishi had issued for the A6M fighter? The answer is yes! The person owning that aircraft was a personal friend of Amelia's. In fact, she and Paul Mantz had recorded the speed records. For the

Japanese, the question became, "How could the plans for this aircraft be obtained?"

Howard Hughes designed and built the H-1 racer in 1935. In addition to setting the world records, it had also set a transcontinental speed record across the United States. It has been reported that when the H-1 arrived in Newark, New Jersey, at the conclusion of this flight that Japanese officials were there, obviously wanted to look at the H-1. Quite possibly one of them could have been Horikoshi, who was working nearby at the Curtiss-Wright plant.

Certainly these officials would have wanted to talk with Hughes. There is a connection here, Horikoshi already knew Amelia Earhart. At some point he would have learned that she and Hughes were friends and that she had assisted during the speed trials of the H-1.

I consider the following a sad story. The United States military was interested in the H-1. General Henry "Hap" Arnold, as their representative flew to California to see the plane. For some reason Hughes' security people would not let him in the hangar. Furious, Arnold returned to Washington, having no more interest in the H-1. Meanwhile, an inferior aircraft, the Buffalo FA2 continued to be built by the Brewster Aeronautical Corporation.

During the Battle of Midway, more than twenty of these Buffalos were sent to intercept the incoming Japanese. Pilots flying Zeros shot down all of them in a few minutes of the battle. The Buffalos, no match for the Zero, become nothing more than flying coffins, all because some security people had refused to allow General Arnold to inspect the H-1 some years earlier. It is reported that more than four hundred American pilots died fighting the Zero during the first few months of WWII. Most probably, had Arnold been allowed in the hangar, this would not have occurred.

The question becomes: How did Mitsubishi obtain plans for the H-1? No one knows for sure. Hughes had business interests in Japan. He was also concerned about his friend Amelia, knowing that she had been captured while spying and could be subject to execution.

A friend of Joe Gervais had received a letter from a Mr. Gibson, who had seen Earhart's file at the State Department. One of his comments was that he had seen a photograph taken in the fall of

1939 of Earhart and Chuichi Nagumo, who later became an Admiral, taken during the wind tunnel test on the Zero. As stated earlier, Earhart had flown the tests for that aircraft. Shortly, thereafter, production began so these could be put on Japanese carriers. Remember, this was in 1939, two years before the attack on Pearl Harbor.

It is known that the State Department had a complete file on Earhart's activities in Japan. How had the true information been acquired by the State Department? Had it come form the Ambassador who could travel throughout Japan and was, most probably, keeping an eye on Amelia? Or at least until his internment by the Japanese on December 8, 1941. Had it come from representatives of the Vatican, including Cardinal Spellman, who had access to all the Catholic churches in Japan?

What is amazing and almost unbelievable is that the United States military apparently remained clueless regarding the onset of the Zero. Pilots in China, known as the Flying Tigers, who had been fighting for the Chinese reportedly sent reports about the Japanese fighters they were facing. Apparently, our military did not believe that a plane with such speed and acuity could be build in Japan and ignored the reports from those actually fighting the Zero. Only after a Zero was shot down in the Aleutians and was secured did our military realize what a superb aircraft it was.

In 1947, when Howard Hughes was testifying in Washington, he admitted under oath that his record-breaking H-1 had been the prototype for the Mitsubishi Zero. Without the zero, the Japanese would not have had sufficient air superiority to risk war with the United States. Hughes testified before a Senate Committee investigating his wartime contracts, that, "I was told that the Japanese copied the Zero from the H-1."

Even though Hughes ended his testimony by defiantly walking out on the Senate hearing, no contempt charge was ever filed and no United States Senator cross-examined him about how the Japanese had obtained the plans. Wouldn't the Senators have been surprised to learn that Amelia Earhart had been living in the Imperial Palace at the pleasure of the Emperor?

The A6M, known by Americans as the Zero, had a maximum speed of 340 miles an hour and could reach 26,250 feet in 9 minutes and 57 seconds. Several variants were added to this most successful of fighters, including a fire extinguisher. Also, the original models did not have rubberized fuel tanks and could be set afire easily with a direct hit on the tanks.

The Hughes racer had a top speed of 351 miles per hour. The Zero came close to that speed, but a difference in weight and armament could have made the difference.

Without the Zero, the Japanese could not have attacked Pearl Harbor on December 7, 1941. But, there is much more to the history of planning of that attack. It should be mentioned that Roosevelt apparently had to have known about the attack in advance, as detailed in Robert Stinnett's book *Day of Deceit*. Also, military personnel who knew and could have warned Short and Kimmel in Hawaii may have wanted to, but were forcibly restrained from doing so. But, how did the attack come about and who planned and orchestrated the details?

# 13 AMELIA EARHART AND PEARL HARBOR

When I started this project, I never thought that Pearl Harbor research would be needed. I was wrong.

At nine years of age, I was listening to the radio that fateful Sunday afternoon when the program was interrupted with an announcement that the Japanese bombed the Hawaiian Islands. I had no idea where they were. The next day I heard President Roosevelt's Day of Infamy speech to Congress. Based on what I now know, the President had deceived the American people.

Early in my research, I received a document from Irene Bolman's sister-in-law also named Irene. It was a summary of Joe Gervais' last meeting with Paul Briand, author of *Daughter of the Sky*, which had been published in 1960. He became the first Earhart scholar to write about the Japanese connection. Briand was quite ill, but Gervais wanted to meet with him one last time. Briand said that what happened to Amelia Earhart lies with her sister Muriel, Jackie Cochran and Margaret Haviland Putnam Lewis, who was George Putnam's fourth and last wife.

During that last meeting, Briand told Gervais the following:

The truth is so horrible and disgusting, that is, nobody can tell it. I am perfectly willing to believe with you that she survived eight years of Japanese protection and returned to this country with a new identity of Irene Craigmile, as stated in the book *Amelia Earhart Lives* by Joe Klaas. But I don't believe that Amelia Earhart continued as a heroine, and that is why things are so hush-hush. It is a terrible truth that everybody is trying to hide. If it were a heroic truth, it would have been exploited long before this. Let us, therefore, clear the cobwebs from our minds. Like you, I am convinced that she did end up in Saipan. I do believe she was on a spy mission, and I concur with your investigations throughout the Pacific. What happened after that, however, sets a fiction writer's imagination ablaze.

In a White Paper issued by Secretary of State Cordell Hull in January 1943, Joseph Grew, the Ambassador in Japan, revealed that the Japanese not only planned a year in advance for a "surprise mass attack on Pearl Harbor," but did their diplomatic utmost to maneuver Japanese-American peace discussions in such a way that President Roosevelt would be in the hands of the Japanese Navy when the attack came. Grew warned the State Department as early as January 27, 1941 that the Japanese planned a surprise attack. Until September 23, 1941, Japanese diplomats had persisted in trying to lure the President onto a Japanese battleship in the Pacific for a "Peace Conference." If Hull agreed to the idea, the country would have suffered an even greater national humiliation than what eventually occurred. After much pressure and veiled threats, the Japanese gave up on the idea of kidnapping the President, according to Grew. Later, they sent Ambassador Saburo Kurusu as a special "peace" emissary to Washington, where he waved the olive branch along with Ambassador Nomura while Japanese planes crept closer to Pearl Harbor.

This country has lived with the Pearl Harbor syndrome for years because of two dates, July 2, 1937 and December 7, 1941. They are bound by a single thread, which connects these events. After a change of nationality to Japan as of 1939, America's First Lady of the Air would help plan, execute and lead an attack that would shake this nation to its very core. She became Air Marshall Earhart, Chief of Staff to the Japanese Imperial Air Force and was called a woman who dared.

Before he died in 1977, Admiral Chester A. Nimitz, Commander of all naval forces in the Pacific during World War II, states the following during an interview with Fred Goerner, a friend and AE researcher who worked at CBS. "When truth is revealed about Amelia Earhart, it will stagger the imagination of the American people."

How did Briand obtain this new information after having written *Daughter of the Sky*? I believe it came from Mitsuo Fuchida, who led the attack on Pearl Harbor. Later he became a Christian and spent much time in the United States during the 1960's. Fuchida would have worked closely with Amelia Earhart during the planning phase of the attack and its execution at Pearl Harbor.

After the Japanese attacked Russia on June 22, 1941, a controversy escalated between the Army and the Navy. The Army wanted to attack Russia from Manchuria. The Navy wanted to attack Pearl Harbor in order to keep the trade routes open to the East Indies without interference from the United States Navy. Roosevelt wanted the Japanese to attack Pearl Harbor to force the United States into the war. Earhart was a close associate of Yamamoto. Did FDR get word to her to do her best to assist the Japanese Navy in winning the argument concerning Pearl Harbor? He had ways of contacting her via our Embassy or through Cardinal Spellman, who made regular visits to Japan.

The day after the attempt to get President Roosevelt aboard a Japanese battleship concluded on September 23, 1941, Japanese officials sent a Bomb Plot map to Japanese intelligence officers on Hawaii. There were five blocks on each map, each indicating an area of Hawaii. Personnel were ordered to monitor daily what was happening in each area and report to Japan. Although the United States had broken the Japanese code and was decoding messages, none of this information was sent to Kimmel or Short. In fact, the Chief of Naval Intelligence, Captain Alan G. Kirk, who had been appointed in March 1941, was replaced in October because he insisted on warning those in charge in Hawaii. Certainly, he had been warned of the consequences should he remain determined to do so.

The United States addressed the decoded Bomb Plot messages to the "Chief of 3rd Bureau, Naval General Staff" and marked them as Secret Intelligence Messages. They were given special serial numbers so the significance could not be missed. The message sent to Japanese Intelligence officers in Hawaii is as follows:

Henceforth, we would like to have you make reports concerning vessels along the following lines insofar as possible:

1. The waters (of Pearl Harbor) are to be divided roughly into five sub-areas. (We have no objection to your abbreviating as much as you like.)

Area A. Waters between Ford Island and the Arsenal.

Area B. Waters adjacent to the island south and west of the Ford Island. (This area is on the opposite of the island from Area A.)

Area C. East Loch.

Area D. Middle Loch.

Area E. West Loch and the Communication water routes.

2. With regard to warships and aircraft carriers, we would like you have you report on those anchor (These are not so important.), tied up at wharves, buoys and docks. (Designate types and classes briefly. If possible we would like to have you mention when there are two or more vessels along the same wharf.)

When I first read the Bomb Plot, I could see Amelia's influence. The wording had less of a military tone, but was written by someone who was intelligent and highly organized. She was an American female writing to Japanese intelligence officers. Even though she was the Commander of the Japanese Air Force, she no doubt had to be careful in how they worked together. All involved knew she was very close to the Admiral Yamamoto, so the feeling might have been, "You better do what she says."

Per orders from Washington, General Short and Admiral Kimmel never received any of the Bomb Plot messages that were obtained between September 24th and December 7th. Although they were sent in J-19 and PA-K2 codes, which were less secret than the ones in the Purple Code, Commander Joseph L. Rochefort could have read them at any time. He had been sent to Pearl Harbor in early 1941 as the officer in charge of Station Hypo. Rochefort was an expert Japanese linguist and trained cryptanalyst.

These Bomb Plot messages, as have been shown, designate Pearl Harbor as the first target of any Japanese attack. If these messages had been read by Rochefort, they would have been more of a warning of a direct Japanese threat to Pearl Harbor than the Purple and diplomatic messages, some of which actually encourages top naval authorities in Washington to believe that war with Japan would probably start in the Far East.

As stated earlier, Paul Briand was so upset with the information concerning Amelia Earhart, he ended further research and stated that she planned, implemented and led the attack on Pearl Harbor. Who best knew Pearl Harbor? With Japanese aircraft participating in the attack, she needed to be with them.

One distinguished Earhart researcher has claimed that Earhart surfaced in a Japanese I-Class submarine that carried a seaplane, took off from near Niihau Island, met the incoming Japanese strike force from the carriers and flew as lead plane over Pearl Harbor. After leading the strike force, she landed near the submarine and was returned to Japan.

During her transport to Hawaiian waters, I believe Earhart would have been with Captain Kijiro Imaizumi, Commander of the Second Division Submarine, which led the Japanese Task Force. His group included the I-19, I-21 and I-23, all large submarines capable of carrying a seaplane. Prior to heading southeast, he received secret orders to make a special stop. In Burl Burlingame's book *Advance Force-Pearl Harbor*, he wrote that Imaizumi's division was considered a special group. Before he left Japan, Commander Ryunoskuke Arizuni of Naval General Staff sent the three submarines to Hitokappu Bay, there to receive secret orders. Does this confirm a suspicion that he was to pick up Amelia Earhart? Amelia would have been taken to the Hawaiian Islands quietly and secretly.

Her mission complete, Earhart returned to Japan via submarine and was soon at work in her office at Dai Ichi building. With Japan at war with the United States, President Roosevelt is pleased. Admiral Yamamoto is not pleased and felt that the failure of the Japanese diplomats to notify the United States before the attack and about the attack itself, had only "awakened a sleeping giant."

# 14 PRESIDENT ROOSEVELT AND PEARL HARBOR

This chapter will be difficult to write, but I will report the information as best as I can. Telling a story of how a few men were responsible for the deaths of thousands and covered it up since 1941 will make it difficult to believe. These men went down in history as some of the greatest leaders. One of them, General George C. Marshall, told his men that they would have to take what happened to their graves and they did.

The Germans attacked Russia on June 22, 1941. The code name was "Barbarosa." Upon hearing the news, Roosevelt was so upset that he was confined to bed for a month. He had once applied for membership in the Communist Party, but his advisors discouraged that. He knew, however, that something had to be done to help Stalin. America had to enter the war.

For more than a year, Roosevelt had sent American ships into the Atlantic to cause an incident that would upset citizens so much that they would be willing to enter the war. That never happened. He had to try something else.

The United States had been warned by the governments of Great Britain, the Netherlands, Australia, Peru, Korea and the Soviet Union that a surprise attack on Pearl Harbor was coming. FDR, General Marshall and other military officials knew that this was going to happen, allowed it and kept it a secret. FDR had also known from our MAGIC code intercepts, that if Japan attacked the United States and was successful, then Hitler would declare war on this nation. If Japan attacked Pearl Harbor, it had to look as if the Pacific fleet had been destroyed. If Japan attacked the Philippines, however, it had to appear that they could win a conflict without difficulty. The problem was how to maneuver the Japanese into firing the first shot. Japan had to succeed or Hitler would renege on his stated intention.

War with Japan was seen as inevitable, because they had to attack the Philippines. According to Mark Emerson Willey, author of *Pearl Harbor – Mother of All Conspiracies*, if the Japanese fleet was destroyed, it would defeat the purpose. It would be obvious suicide for Hitler to declare war if Japan were crippled. That would allow the United States to attack him without even the possibility of a two-front war. The plan would work only if Japan were successful with attacks on both Pearl Harbor and the Philippines. The lure of a weakened United States in a two-front war focused on Japan seemed to make a German Declaration of War cost-free. It was a trap, however, because FDR was always going to ignore Japan and go after Hitler, the ultimate goal being to protect the Soviet Union.

One of the first actions FDR took after Hitler attacked Russia was to have all intelligence obtained in the Pacific arena sent to Washington and not be shared with Admiral Kimmel or General Short in Hawaii. The argument in Japan was whether to have the Army invade Russia or the Navy to attack the United States Pacific fleet to ensure the supply of goods that came through the Dutch East Indies. Had Amelia Earhart swayed the decision for the naval plan? A better understanding of what had occurred would probably have been in the papers that Jackie Cochran and Cardinal Spellman took from Amelia's office in August 1945 but never made public.

In addition to the Bomb Plot warnings, another advance notice, referred to as the "Red Cross Connection," was put into action, which was written by Daryl S. Borquist.

Don C. Smith, who directed the War Services for the Red Cross before WWII, was Deputy Administrator of Services to the Armed Forces from 1942 to 1946. Apparently, when he had become the Administrator, he knew about the advance plans concerning Pearl Harbor. After his death in 1990, his daughter Helen E. Hamman saw the news coverage efforts by the families of Husband Kimmel and Walter Short to restore their deserved ranks. She wrote a letter to President Clinton on September 5, 1995, recalling a conversation she had with her father.

Shortly before the attack in 1941, President Roosevelt called Smith to the White House for a meeting concerning a Top Secret matter. Hamman wrote, "At this meeting the President advised my father that his intelligence staff had informed him of a pending attack on Pearl Harbor by the Japanese. He anticipated many casualties and much loss. He instructed my father to send workers and supplies to a holding area at a point of entry on the west coast where they would await orders to ship out. No destination was revealed. FDR left no doubt in my father's mind that none of the naval and other military officials in Hawaii were to be informed and he was not to advise the Red Cross officers who were already in the area. When he (my father) protested, President Roosevelt told him that the American people would never agree to enter the war in Europe unless they were attacked.

My father was privy to Top Secret operations and worked directly with our outstanding leaders. He followed presidential orders, but spent many years contemplating actions, which he considered ethically and morally wrong.

It is estimated that Red Cross supplies worth $70,000 were sent to Hawaii in 1941 prior to Pearl Harbor. Workers ordered there hurriedly established ten emergency medical stations.

Another story, interesting because of its implications, is found in David's Bergamini's *Japan's Imperial Conspiracy– How Hirohito Led Japan into War Against the West*. On November 2, 1941, after a tiring day of listening to Prime Minister Hideki Tojo explain the planned attack on Pearl Harbor, as opposed to Russia or the West Indies, Hirohito made the following statement, "I suggest that we send a special envoy to the Pope so we can use him as a mediator to save the situation if worst comes to worst." The Emperor asked several shrewd questions, but finally gave Tojo approval for the contact to be made. Thus, he approved of attacking Pearl Harbor and going to war earlier rather than later and issued the orders.

Knowing Japan was not going to attack Russia, allowed Stalin to move his Siberian troops, with all their winter equipment, to St. Petersburg in time to save the city. The Germans were totally surprised and retreated. Some historians consider this event as the turning point in Russia's war with Germany.

At 10:15 a.m. on November 15, 1941, General Marshall revealed one of this nation's most vital secrets – United States cryptologists could read Japan's coded messages. Inconceivably, he did not request the presence of Short or Kimmel, the two men in charge of the military in Hawaii, nor did he give them a separate briefing. Stinnett discloses that secrets denied to Short and Kimmel were shared with four media and three wire services. Those selected to represent the media complied with the secrecy rules. They were Robert Sherrold, *Time Magazine*; Ernest Lindley, *Newsweek Magazine*; Charles Hurd, *New York Times*; Bert Andrews, *New York Herald Tribune*; Lyle Wilson, *United Press International*; Edward Bomar, *Associated Press* and Harold Slater, *International News Service*. Thousands were going to die and these media representatives remained silent.

Another story relevant to the days before Pearl Harbor involved a Dutch submarine that had visually tracked the Japanese fleet to the Kurile Islands in November 1941. This information was sent to Washington, but nothing was forwarded to Hawaii.

On November 25th, the Navy ordered all United States trans-Pacific shipping to take a southern route. All long-range PBY patrols from the Aleutians were ordered to stop on December 6th to prevent any contact with the Japanese attack fleet.

The Japanese Strike Force, however, was NOT keeping radio silence. More than 663 radio messages were heard between November 16th and December 7th.

John Toland, author of *Infamy: Pearl Harbor and It's Aftermath*, spent two years searching for witnesses of events. Finally he located Admiral Johann Ranneft, who in 1941 had been a Captain serving as the Dutch Naval Attaché to the United States. The Captain wrote that he frequently was allowed into the Naval Intelligence office in San Francisco. On December 3, he was told that they had tracked the location of the Japanese carriers from their radio transmissions. When he returned on December 6th and asked where the fleet was, a man pointed to an area 200 miles from Pearl Harbor.

This claim contradicts the sanctioned version of history, in which it is declared that "Admiral Nagumo's Task Force left Kuriles on November 26th and arrived undetected at a point about 200 miles north of Oahu at 0600 hours (Hawaiian Time) on December 7th."

Contrary to the movie *Tora, Tora, Tora* during the night of December 6th, Roosevelt along with top advisors Harry Hopkins, Henry Stimson, George Marshall, Secretary of the Navy Knox and aides John McGrea and Frank Beatty deliberately waited through the night for the Japanese to strike Pearl Harbor.

According to Admiral Paulus P. Powell, he and other Naval Intelligence officers were kept under armed guard for fear they might try to contact Hawaii before the attack. If they had, they would have been shot. Admiral Powell told his story to Lyle Hartford Van Dyke, Sr. whose uncle had sent a key intelligence message to Washington, which was promptly secured.

About the same time, General "Hap" Arnold, Chief of the Army Air Forces was sent to Hamilton Field in California arriving from Washington only an hour before he was to release thirteen B-17s. The B-17s were to arrive at Oahu at exactly 8:00 a.m., the same time the Japanese had planned to attack. Looking into the faces of the men he was probably sending to their deaths, he lamely warned them that, "War is imminent and you may run into a war during your flight."

Major Truman H. Landon asked the natural question, "If we are going into war, why don't we have machine guns?" The bomber crews weren't allowed ammunition and the guns were packed in cosmoline.

Three observations were made concerning the B-17s:

1. The Honolulu music radio station KGMB was turned on all night, at a cost to the Army, which signaled all the islands that the American planes were coming in.
2. It was also an attempt to confuse the radar controllers, which in fact it did.
3. It caused additional damage to our heavy bomber fleet.

The fact that the bombers would fly on a Sunday was unusual and that they would arrive exactly at 8:00 a.m., the time scheduled for the attack is highly unusual and suspicious. The Chief of the Army Air Forces was sent from Washington to time their departure from California was an impossible coincidence.

When the B-17s arrived near Hawaii, the pilots thought they were being met with a fighter escort, only to find that the approaching aircraft were Japanese fighters. The order was given to disperse and find alternate airfields. All landed with only slight damage to some of the aircrafts.

The carrier *Enterprise* was returning to Pearl Harbor after delivering planes to Wake Island. Bad weather had delayed the ship. Thus making it safe from the Japanese attack, along with the newest support ships: *Northampton, Chester,* and *Salt Lake City* and nine destroyers all being commanded by Vice Admiral William F. Halsey.

On Friday, December 5th, the carrier *Lexington* commanded by Rear Admiral John H. Newton had been ordered to leave Pearl Harbor. The *Lexington* took on some aircrafts with indication of delivering them to Midway Island. Heavy cruisers *Chicago, Portland* and *Astoria* as well as five destroyers went with the carrier. Instead of going to Midway, the ships cruised southwest of Pearl Harbor until the attack was over.

What was important was that the heavy cruisers could travel at 32.7 knots, allowing them to stay with the carriers; which cruised at about 33 knots. Capable of only 18 knots, the battleships had been left at Pearl Harbor to endure the attack. What may not have been widely circulated was that the new *Iowa* class battleships were already being built and would be on line by late 1942.

After the Pearl Harbor attack and even before getting the after battle report, FDR called Lord Halifax at the British Embassy telling him that the Japanese were bombing Pearl Harbor. He asked him to pass it on as quickly as he could to London.

At midnight on December 7th, FDR met with OSS Director William Donavan and CBS newsman Edward R. Morrow. Having seen many statesmen in crisis, the latter was surprised at FDR's calm reaction. After reviewing the latest news from Pearl Harbor, FDR tested Morrow's instinct for news with two bizarre questions. "Did this surprise you?" Morrow said it had. FDR countered with, "Maybe you think it didn't surprise us?" FDR gave the impression that the attack itself was not unwelcome.

Admiral Nimitz flew to Hawaii to assume command of the Pacific Fleet, arriving on Christmas Eve 1941. There was such a feeling of despair; dejection and defeat that you would have thought the Japanese had already won the war. The Admiral received a tour of the destruction wrought on Pearl Harbor. Sunken battleships and other naval vessels clutters the waters everywhere we looked.

As the tour boat returned to the dock, the young helmsman asked, "Well, Admiral, what do you think after seeing all this destruction?" Nimitz shocked everyone within hearing distance by the sound of his voice. He said, "The Japanese made three of the biggest mistakes an attack force could ever make or God was taking care of America. Which do you think it was?"

Nimitz explained:

Mistake Number One: The Japanese attacked on a Sunday. Nine out of every ten crewmen of those ships were ashore on leave. If they had been aboard and the ships sunk, we would have lost 38,000 men instead of 3,800.

Mistake Number Two: When the Japanese saw all those battleships lined in a row, they got so carried away sinking those ships, they never once bombed our dry docks opposite those ships. If they had destroyed our dry docks, we would have had to tow every one of those ships to America to be repaired. As it is now, the ships are in shallow water and can be raised. One tug can pull them over to the dry docks and we can have them repaired and at sea by the time we could have towed them to America. I already have crews ashore anxious to man those ships.

Mistake Number Three: Every drop of fuel in the Pacific Theater is in the top of the ground storage tanks five miles away over the hill. One attack plane could have strafed those tanks and destroyed our fuel supply. That's why I say the Japanese made three of the biggest mistakes an attack force could make. God was taking care of America.

It is believed President Roosevelt had chosen the right man for the job. With all the dejection, despair and defeat in the air, the U.S. needed someone who could see the silver lining.

After reading the above comments, I reviewed the Japanese Attack Plan and it had to have been prepared by Amelia Earhart. She would not let any small detail go unnoticed. Every Japanese pilot had his assignment. I found no flight crew assigned to the dry docks or fuel tanks. Why is that? The only logical conclusion is that these two areas were deliberately ignored. Did the Japanese do this for possible use at a later date, or had it been a meeting of the minds between Earhart and Roosevelt?

In June 1942, the Japanese had sent more than 100,000 troops as part of the attack on Midway. Was it possible that the Japanese had been thinking of invading Hawaii after destroying our carrier force during the attack? As it happened, the enemy lost four of the carriers used during the Pearl Harbor attack and one heavy cruiser, which had demoralizing blows.

I have some personal questions. Information exists that Amelia Earhart, who planned the attack on Pearl Harbor, was to be delivered by submarine or possibly the I-19, so she could join the attack force and lead it to Pearl Harbor. The I-19 carried a seaplane. Mitsuo Fuchida was flying a Mitsubishi Type 97 bomber. Could Earhart's seaplane have kept up with him, or would the Japanese have had another plane waiting on Niihau for her? Would one of the Attack Force aircraft have stopped for her? In Amelia's possessions on July 2, 1982 was a map of Niihau, which was later, published in some books. The map showed the island with two runways drawn on it. The Robinson family, who had watched her takeoff from Oakland in March 1937, owned the island. Amelia had met them just before her first world flight attempt. The family was also on very friendly terms with Roosevelt. Visitors were not allowed on the island. A good question would be, had Earhart notified the Robinsons that she was going to Niihau Island? If so, had the Robinsons and FDR been in contact? The answer to that may never be proven.

# 15 TOKYO ROSE – THE COVER UP

Let's get something out of the way right now – the first Tokyo Rose was Amelia Earhart. When the subject of Tokyo Rose came up during interviews by Earhart researchers on Saipan, they were told that Amelia Earhart was known as "Tokyo Rosa," which meant "American Spy Girl." That's all, nothing more. The term Tokyo Rose referred to something else.

President Gerald Ford later pardoned Iva Toguri, unjustly convicted of treason for being a Tokyo Rose. This is her story.

Iva spent her childhood days in Los Angeles and graduated from the University of California, Los Angeles in 1941. In July of that year, her aunt's illness sent her; an American citizen to Japan where she was stranded after Pearl Harbor was bombed. With the United States and Japan at war, the Japanese considered her an enemy. She became one of thirteen women, all native speakers of American English and collectively known as Tokyo Rose. During November 1943, she began announcing for the "Zero Hour," an English language propaganda program beamed at United States troops. By this time she had married Felipe J. Aquino.

When Joe Klaas and Joe Gervais were in the Chicago area during their book tour in 1971 to publicize, they realized Iva Toguri Aguino lived there. After locating her, they visited with her for nine hours. The following is from that interview. Klaas opened the conversation by saying; "I have found no evidence after reading your trial transcript that you ever identified yourself as Tokyo Rose on Japanese radio."

"No, I only called myself 'Little Orphan Annie' on the air," the worry-worn slender woman who had just spent six years in a Federal Prison in West Virginia replied. "Once during a broadcast I even got arrested by Japan's Kempti, the secret police because I played the *Stars and Stripes Forever* on my program the day the United States Marines invaded Saipan. The police mistook it for our *Star Spangled Banner*. I'm Nisei, an American-born United States Citizen."

"But were you convicted of treason?" Klaas asked.

"I am not a traitor!" She snapped. "I only took a job spinning American records on Japanese radio to earn a living after U.S. authorities failed to repatriate me. But, as I commented, no treason ever! I'm as patriotic an American as you are."

"Then, why were you convicted?"

"It was Walter Winchell," she replied.

"What?!" Klaas exclaimed.

"Winchell made me a 'scoop' for his newspaper column." Her eyes misted. "I did tell a magazine that I might be 'Tokyo Rose' because all of us, American and British women who broadcast over Tokyo radio were nicknamed 'Tokyo Rose' by Allied soldiers who listened to them. Any female voice broadcasting in English from Japan was called Tokyo Rose. It was a name our troops dreamed up, I guess."

Iva continued, "It was Winchell who made it mean traitor. I got stuck with it and spent six years in prison. None of the other women were charged with anything. When I was sent to prison for being a traitor, I became only the one as far as Walter Winchell was concerned. Just unlucky, I guess."

"Or…a wild though just struck me," Klaas exclaimed. "Maybe you were framed as Tokyo Rose to cover up a code-name Tokyo Rosa, which meant 'American Spy Lady' to natives who saw Amelia Earhart alive on Saipan."

"It may not be an answer to any one who hasn't been called a hated name for twenty-five years and served six long years in prison." Iva began to cry. "But to me and my poor father who always said it had to be some elaborate cover-up of something we knew nothing about, what you wrote about Amelia Earhart in *Amelia Earhart Lives* makes sense."

Amelia's husband George Putnam was commissioned a Major and sent on a special assignment. He had made dangerous three-day trek through Japanese territory to reach a Marine Corps radio station near the coast of China where broadcast reception was loud and clear. After listening to the voice for less than a minute, he said decisively, "I'll stake my life that this is not Amelia's voice. It sounds to me as if the woman might have lived in New York and been fiendishly well coached, but Amelia – never."

We know from Iva that there were several woman talking on the English-speaking Japanese radio station. Which one did Putnam hear?

Is it not known within which time frame Earhart was talking on the radio. She became involved in many activities in Japan, however and probably would have had little time to spend on broadcasts.

In Glenn Beck's book, *The Making of America, Miracles and Massacres – True and Untold Stories*, he highlights events at Toguri's trial. One thing he did not know was that Amy Earhart, Amelia's mother attended every court session. She must have known that her daughter had been a Tokyo Rose and wanted to see if her name was mentioned during the trial.

Toguri asked her visitors, "Why is the government protecting her and why was I the scapegoat in the trial?"

Finally, were Walter Winchell's actions also part of a government cover-up? President Truman wanted nothing to do with the trial of Iva Toguri. He had had great difficulty trying to keep the Emperor of Japan from being put on trial. Our Allies had been furious. Hirohito could have been questioned about Earhart's activities in Japan during the war, especially about her living in the Imperial Palace. Her assistance in planning the Pearl Harbor attack also had to be kept secret at all costs.

# 16 EARHART SIGHTINGS

Since the day Amelia Earhart virtually disappeared from public view, reports of her being seen in the Marshall Islands, on Saipan and in Japan have surfaced. It was no secret that she was living at the Imperial Palace and working in the Dai Ichi Military Building. She was seen stopping to view the beautiful flower garden near her office. She was seen around the city and enjoyed many of the fine restaurants.

Michael Seckman, a cousin of Amelia's relates what Abe Jacobs told him. Jacobs was captured in the Philippines, transported to an unmarked hospital ship to Tokyo sometime in late 1942 and remained a POW until the end of the war. To get out of working in the coalmines, where life could be short, he took sandpaper and rubbed himself raw. The Japanese were terrified of venereal disease, which he appeared to have and put him in a hospital in Tokyo.

To pass time, he would look out the window at the passing cars. During his interview with Seckman at the Soldiers and Sailors Home in Quincy, Illinois on July 15, 1982, talk turned to Tokyo Rose. He insisted that she had an American voice some of the time when he heard the broadcasts. The local word was that she had short blondish brown hair.

Jacobs recalled looking out his window on several occasions and seeing Hirohito's motor cavalcade coming down the street. On three occasions he saw a white woman in a white dress riding with him. Once she got out of the car with him to look at the flower garden. She was thin and had short curly brown hair and a pleasant smile. She seemed shy and very mannerly. When Seckman asked the identity of the person, without hesitating Jacobs said, "I think it was Amelia Earhart." Questioned further, he added that everyone seemed to know she was living in the Imperial Palace. Jacobs placed the time as being during the spring of 1943. Abe Jacobs' story is just one example of her being seen and identified.

Another report concerning Earhart comes from a serviceman, who shall remain unnamed. He told the following story to the FBI. The informant related that he had been attached to the American Forces in the Philippines before Pearl Harbor. On one occasion some Japanese in a hotel there entertained him and another solider. He described the walls as being extremely thin, enabling him to hear a conversation in English between two Japanese to the effect that Amelia Earhart was still alive and being detained in a Tokyo hotel

Subsequently, this informant was taken as a prisoner along with others on Bataan. As a POW, he was given the task of typing statements made by American officers to Japanese intelligence authorities. He recalled that one day, after a number of interviews had been conducted, he was alone in the office with a Japanese intelligence officer. He inquired of this man if "my cousin Amelia Earhart was still alive." The officer stated he could tell him nothing except, "Don't worry about her well being. She is perfectly all right."

The following report was given to an Amelia Earhart researcher by an unnamed veteran, who recalled,

The First Marine Division moved into Naha, Okinawa, about fifteen years ago this month. In mopping up operations such as forcing snipers out of hiding, detonating mines and finding booby traps, I called out to see if anyone was there before entering one house, indistinguishable from other vacated residences in the neighborhood. In this house, however, there were Japanese language magazines scattered all over the floor. I stopped for a rest and to have a smoke. I picked up a magazine that resembled in shape and format our *LOOK* magazine, except that there were fewer photos and more writing. One photo, about six inches square, was of Amelia Earhart. She was standing with her back to a plane. By her were Japanese soldiers, with weapons at order, all facing the camera and smiling. Strangely enough, Earhart was also smiling, with that same half-smile that was her trademark.

Jerry Steigmann, a retired New York City detective living in Phoenix, gave the following information to several researchers about Colonel Gregory "Pappy" Boyington. He had been a former Flying Tiger (American Volunteer Group) and had served in China with

Claire Channault prior to Pearl Harbor. He then went back into the United States military services. Flying in a United States Marine Corps air wing, he became commanding officer of the Black Sheep Squadron; a ragtag bunch of foul-ups flying in the South Pacific. Eventually shot down at Rabaul in January 1944, he was picked up by a Japanese submarine and taken to Truk, to Saipan and finally to a top secret Japanese Navy prison camp near Yakohama. According to Marine Corps records, he had died in the Pacific Ocean and received the Medal of Honor posthumously.

Camp Ofuna, a secret Imperial Japanese Navy high-interrogation camp near Yokohama had been the Japanese equivalent to a Hollywood Studio prior to WWII. Prisoners held there were off the books. In other words, the Japanese did not notify the Swiss Red Cross, who would have forwarded information Boyington was alive. He remained missing in action or dead. That is why no one knew of his being alive until fourteen days after the war was over and he was liberated.

Now for the rest of the story! During the 1980's, Boyington attended the Falcon Field Air Show at Mesa, Arizona. Usually present was the former Japanese Navy pilot who claimed he had shot "Pappy" down. The two would argue about their air combat missions, all in a good-natured way.

Steigmann interviewed them jointly and separately about Earhart. They both revealed that she had visited Camp Ofuna with some high-ranking Japanese Naval Air Commanders. She had acted as if she were a dignitary instead of a prisoner.

Steigmann asked "Pappy" if he had ever told anyone about Earhart's visit. He replied, "No one ever asked me and I was the Big Black Sheep of the Marine Corps. No one wanted to hear my opinions or advice about anything. I took my pension and flew away."

This following report deals with intelligence that began to be received by the O.S.S. at their headquarters in Rome soon after it had been freed from the Germans in June 1944. Joseph Persico, author of *Roosevelt's Secret War*, includes the following information.

Soon after the liberation of the Eternal City, the O.S.S. set up a headquarters run by Victor Scamporini, a former State Department official. In mid-1944 a windfall dropped in

76

Scamporini's lap. Through an intermediary named Flilippo Settacioli, he began receiving tantalizing transmissions from within the supposedly impenetrable Vatican.

The first delivery to Scamporini was a copy of a cable from the Pope's Apostle in Tokyo. Soon the Vatican reports began to flow so heavily that one O.S.S. operator was occupied solely with translating and transmitting them to Washington.

Donovan's front office was overjoyed with both the volume and quality of intelligence being received. During January 1945, these reports were assigned a special code word "vessel" and were classified top secret/control, which meant that only those on a restricted list could see this intelligence.

The reason that this intelligence flowing to the O.S.S. is included in this book is that it needs to be examined to a greater degree. Was Amelia Earhart involved in gathering and sharing this intelligence from Tokyo? Was Cardinal Spellman the Pope's Apostle Delegate in Tokyo?

When Jackie Cochran and Cardinal Spellman visited with General MacArthur in the Philippines before going to Tokyo to get Amelia's files the subject of intelligence was broached. After that meeting, MacArthur did not advocate the Emperor being tried as a war criminal. Was it the intelligence flowing from the Vatican or did it have more to do with the whole Amelia Earhart situation? This including her living in the Imperial Palace and the things she had done in Japan is what the United States did not want to make public.

The General had his own problems to deal with by allowing his forces to be destroyed, per orders from Roosevelt as part of the Pearl Harbor fiasco. He certainly wanted to contain any damaging revelations.

The problem became President Truman's when he had to tell our Allies that the Emperor of Japan would not stand trial. That pronouncement angered them! When fire bombings began devastating areas in Tokyo, concerned persons thought it was time to move Earhart to a safer place.

# 17 EARHART LEAVES TOKYO

On a warm Saturday afternoon in the Mid-Atlantic Museum's Air Show in Reading, Pennsylvania, Colonel Robert Morgan and I took a Pepsi break. As the former pilot of the *Memphis Belle*, he was doing a seminar at the show. I was a member of the National War Plane Museum in Geneseo, New York. For this show we had brought a B-17 and a C-47 to display. My job was handling the tours of the C-47.

During our conversation about nothing in particular and without any preparation, Morgan looked at me and said, "I led the first fire bombing raid on Tokyo." It was if our table had become a confessional and Bob wanted to get something off his chest. The first such raid occurred on November 4, 1944 and leveled four square miles of Tokyo, killing more Japanese than either of the atomic bombs.

I bring up this event as I try to determine when Amelia had been moved from Tokyo for her personal safety. The Japanese government operated the internment camp near Weihsien in China, not the military. In that camp were many priests, nuns and missionaries. The Vatican certainly knew of this camp and may have been active in sending Earhart there. The Chief of the Japanese Consular Service visited the special lady on a daily basis. No doubt his reports were communicated immediately to Japanese authorities and the Emperor. I have to believe Cardinal Spellman was also involved in the whole situation.

Researchers from TIGHAR interviewed those involved in the Office of Strategic Command (O.S.S.), camp administrators and internees. They read camp documents and still failed to confirm or deny that Earhart had been at Weihsien. Operatives in the O.S.S. would say nothing about the Earhart situation at Weihsien. She was housed in the off-limits Japanese section of the camp, so internees in the main section had no reason to venture there.

Cochran and Cardinal Spellman met with Admiral Nimitz on Guam before they went to the Philippines to meet with MacArthur.

This meant that the key players were informed as to what was going on concerning Earhart.

After the Japanese surrendered and before the occupation troops arrived in Tokyo, General Arnold sent Jackie Cochran to make an official investigation of what Japanese women had done in the Imperial Air Force. This was nothing more than a cover to remove Earhart's files from the Dai Ichi Building before the troops arrived.

Cochran tells about her experience at the Dai Ichi Building in her book *The Stars at Noon*.

It was a magnificent building and most impressive. But, I will not forget my first entrance. Just as I walked to the door to pull it open toward me, a high-ranking Japanese officer pushed the door in my face and almost pushed me down. He was a haughty customer, still in uniform and carrying his sword. His action was as startling to the military police on duty as to me. There was not the slightest doubt he had seen me through the glass door and his action was premeditated.

My search of the records found no evidence that the Japanese women had participated on any active war effort or home production. I did, however, find numerous clippings and photographs of Amelia Earhart, Jimmy Doolittle and other American pilots, including myself. There were several files on Amelia.

Of course there would have been files related to Earhart because this is where her office had been when serving as Air Commander and Chief of Staff of the Japanese Air Force.

By the end of the war, Earhart was using her new name, Irene Craigmile. The original ledgers of the Japanese prisoner of war and internment camps are at the Washington Navy Yard. In each of the ledgers is the list of internees at a particular location. In one of the dark green volumes marked, WEIHSIEN in white ink on the binding is a page on which the name Irene Craigmile appeared. The entries were made in consistently excellent handwriting, as if someone were transcribing them from a list.

Jim Hannon was one of seven specialists who parachuted into Weihsien to rescue the internees after the war ended. He wrote the following in his report on the mission:

A pre-dawn takeoff followed by a parachute landing and later a monumental discovery was the beginning, followed by five remarkable weeks. At first we were revered and idolized. Then we lost our wings, revealing we were people like them after all. I was familiar with prisoner of war camps, four of the German variety.

The people at Weihsien were Allied Nationals – men, women and children, sun tanned, wearing clean clothes and showing no signs of physical abuse; high spirits and enthusiasm abounded.

Some of the shakers and movers of a world that went down with the United States fleet at Pearl Harbor. In view of what was to follow, our jump into the cornfield opposite the main gate of the Weihsien Internment Camp was an accident in time and place.

The mission was a continuation of my journey that began in Morocco, then in order of Italy, Poland, Czechoslovakia, Hungary, Washington D.C and China with a mission in Hunan Province and finally Weihsien.

What I found in Weihsien reached something in my conscience. A force, subliminal perhaps in the beginning, took root. I state emphatically, nothing herein is intended to be self-serving. To play down the result of my efforts would be self-deprecating and in so doing, would constitute a cover-up of critical facts.

Our leader's, Major Steiger, decisions were final, adhering to our purpose as issued by General Wedemeyer, yet they were not set in concrete; he ruled against those holding special interests.

John Broder, an internee, in due course, provided the key, followed by a broad panel of credible people who, all together, endorsed my conviction that the "Yank" was Amelia Earhart.

Amelia lived in an age when her achievements were international in scope. I found her alive in Weihsien Internment Camp. For a period of four weeks, I saw her virtually every day. Occasionally, more than once, standing beside the bed, leaning over her, I touched her, her eyes locked with mine, I heard her voice.

The facts chronicled in Amelia Earhart 1945 are not hearsay. They are not second or third person and they are not in conflict with evidence gathered before or after Weihsien. I submit Amelia Earhart vanished; she did not die as officially announced.

A priest arrived at Weihsien and had the following discussion with Lt. Hannon:

He looked at me and asked if I knew of a John Birch. I told him an American missionary had known him. I understood his family was permanent China residents. He said Captain Birch was born in China. It was his lifelong and revered home. Birch was intensely loyal to the National Government and an avowed anti-communist who would not permit interrogation by a rebel officer and for that he was executed. He paused for a few minutes and then went on. He had met Birch on his travels. When Captain Birch had asked where he was going, the priest mentioned Weihsien, Tsingtao and Tientsen. The captain told him there was a VIP in Weihsien. VIP was short for "very important person." Weihsien was his immediate target and the presence of a lady VIP there had been confirmed. He wanted to make himself available for any assistance he might render.

I explained my conclusions regarding "Jane Doe" and told him I had released her to a NRA agent named Ingersoll. He had taken her away in a Japanese Betty bomber. His answer insinuated I had not served her well.

In jest, I said, "Whose side are you on, Father?" I wish I hadn't. He said he was on God's side. My response worsened the situation. I said he might be a communist spy disguised as a Catholic priest. He stood up, raised his bag, a little sad. He said his faith and love rested with God and his martyred son Jesus Christ. Father Joyce fastened his eyes on mine, his voice was deliberate, "You were described by a rebel, and a communist and he gave you what you asked of him."

He offered his hand, his smile back in place. I asked if the lady VIP was Amelia Earhart. His answer came as we walked out the gate, "Captain John Birch believed she was."

Amelia was flown to Pusan, Korea dressed as a nun traveling with a group of nuns. This was a way to keep spying eyes away from her. A B-29 flew her to the United States and Bethesda Hospital. After examinations and an operation, she was sent to Maryknoll Seminary in Ossining, New York. Someone used good thinking since Amelia had owned a home in Rye. It would be familiar country for her recovery and recuperation.

Was Amelia a traitor or truly working as a double agent for FDR? Amelia later told Monsignor Kelly that she was upset that she had gotten involved in certain activities while in Japan. Was it really known what type of pressures she had endured while living there? What was known about her being drugged and becoming addicted to narcotics at Weihsien? What effect did all of this truly have on her activities there? What is important in this saga is the role the Vatican played not only while she was in Japan but also her travels back to the United States.

Because of these revelations, I have to believe that Amelia Earhart had been taken to Weihsien Internee Camp to get her out of Tokyo and had been flown back to the United States.

# 18 IRENE CRAIGMILE AND IRENE BOLAM

Most likely, Amelia, now known as Irene Craigmile, having taken the identity of the original Irene O'Crowley Craigmile was taken to the Maryknoll Seminary to recuperate from her years in Japan. Maryknoll, the name coming from a hill near the village is shared by three organizations. One is the Maryknoll Sisters, who are housed in a third building across the road from the main seminary and another building. Founded in 1911, the seminary became known for global nurturing by interacting with people to build churches, schools and orphanages and entering into their daily lives. One country was Japan and the Sisters there assisted Amelia in returning to the United States.

One of the earlier photos of Irene Craigmile published after her leaving Maryknoll appeared in the newspaper serving Great Neck, New York. In the caption, she was described as an Assistant Vice-President of the Great Neck National Bank.

Irene married Guy Bolam in 1958. From the Isle of Wight, he was involved in British intelligence circles. Since returning from Japan, Irene kept close relationships with some people, particularly those in aviation. In the Eisenhower Library in Abilene, Kansas are several letters to and from her friend Barry Goldwater; who was also in communication with Jackie Cochran. Irene seemed to know the most famous people in aviation in the United States. Even our astronauts met her, some not always knowing at first that they were talking with Amelia Earhart, but were later informed by their superiors.

* * * *

On November 28, 1973, a Marine wrote the following letter to Paul Briand:

(DI) I just finished reading a newspaper article in the *Long Island Press* concerning your biography of Amelia Earhart. It reminded me of a couple incidents I was involved in during 1952 or 1953 when I was stationed at Camp LeJeune, North Carolina.

One weekend I went to visit my grandfather at Sanford, North Carolina. On that weekend he was having a party at his home for Captain Robert Oliver Daniel Sullivan, who had been a pilot of the old *China Clipper* (M-130 flying boat operated by Pan American Airways). A large group of pilots and former pilots were there. During the party, I was talking to two women when a man walked up and said to one of them, "Do you know that you look like Amelia Earhart?" The woman replied, "I have been told that before" and laughed it off.

I hardly thought of this until several years later when I was attending Naval Intelligence School in Washington, D.C. Somehow during an informal talk session, after one of my classes, the subject turned to the disappearance of Amelia Earhart, at which time I related the incident in Sanford a number of years before.

As we were leaving the classroom a Rear Admiral, Ret., who had been sitting in on a number of our classes, stopped me and told me it would be a good idea if I forgot about the incident in Sanford.

Because I am still on active duty in the Marine Corps, I would like you to keep my name in confidence concerning this letter.

* * * *

Researcher Charles Hill, however, found that knowing too much about Amelia could cause problems. At the conference of the Amelia Earhart Research Consortium at Purdue University in 1989, he lectured about her world flight, her rescue by the Japanese and her return to this country. As a result, he was fired from his job after being told by his employer that he was a security risk. This was confirmed years later when he received a call from the then-retired Central Intelligence Agency agent who had turned him into the Government. The agent apologized for what had happened.

* * * *

Diana Dawes, one of Irene's friends, reported seeing some interesting items when she visited Irene's home both before and after her death. One day when Irene was not feeling well, she asked Diana to get her hairbrush from the bedroom upstairs. After securing the hairbrush, she looked into one of the closets and saw boxes piled floor to ceiling marked AMELIA EARHART. One can understand Irene wanting personal records in her possession. Were the papers inside still to remain hidden?

Irene kept the fact that she was Amelia Earhart a secret right up to the time she died on July 2, 1982. After that, neighbors reported seeing large black vans with curtained windows arriving at her home and paper shredders being carried inside. Of course, her papers and items relative to Amelia Earhart had to be destroyed or removed and hidden. A year later, when Diana was allowed to enter Irene's home, she found a few items that had not been destroyed. One was the map of Niihau Island with two landing strips sketched on it.

* * * *

Michael Burkert, LTC, U.S. Army, Ret. Sent me the following information concerning his chance meeting with Irene Bolam in 1977. From her conversation, Burkert noted that this woman was more than a simple New Jersey housewife as some people had reported. In this report you will learn about Michael and his father's friend Bill Cole. All my attempts to obtain Cole's military records have failed. They have just disappeared. In this very revealing report by Michael Burkert you will see that Irene had not forgotten Cole and an apparent role he had played in her world flight.

In January 1977 I was a young officer in the U.S. Army. During the course of my leave prior to overseas movement, I accompanied a close friend and fellow officer, who were to deliver his automobile for shipment to Europe. The terminal in those days was in Bayonne, New Jersey. I had previously called my dad at his home and was reminded to look up his old WWII friend Bill Cole. Bill lived in Newark at this time. I made contact with him and was invited to meet him for dinner.

I made my way to Newark, got a hotel room and then called Bill. We decided to meet at a steakhouse for dinner. I took a cab to the address he gave me and we enjoyed a very good dinner and even more enjoyable conversation. Bill was an old friend and had recently retired from commercial flying. In those days commercial airline pilots were required to retire at age 60. He had known my dad since WWII when they were stationed together on Tinian Island, in the Pacific.

Both were B-29 pilots and both flew numerous missions over Japan toward the end of the war. During dinner, Bill asked if I would like to accompany him to a meeting of old-time pilots, he referred to as Early Birds, at the Sheraton Hotel. As I had nothing else to do and always enjoyed "hangar flying" with other pilots, I agreed to go. Bill picked up the check, I paid the tip and we caught a cab to the Sheraton.

When we located the meeting that he had intended to visit, we were told it had ended but everyone had moved to an adjacent room for cocktails. Bill and I went to this room where the Early Birds were having a pretty good time, as pilots are renowned for. They were doing as one would expect pilots to be doing when they aren't flying – enjoying the camaraderie of one's colleagues, accompanied by a lot of talk about flying.

There were around 35 women and men in the room. There was talk of Jacqueline Cochran and I don't know if she had been there or not. I didn't meet her. Some of the pilots weren't so old, as they were WWII pilots and in those days WWII guys like my dad were not that old. There were several former WASP there. I think the Ninety Nines sponsored this meeting as their logo was on the wall and it seemed like most of the ladies present were Ninety Nines.

After securing our adult beverages, we were speaking to a couple that Bill Cole knew and they told him that Irene is here and would be back shortly. Bill told me that I would want to meet Irene as she was a most interesting woman and I wouldn't want to miss her.

Sometime later Irene entered the reception room. The place got very quiet as she walked over toward the bar. It was as if she drew all the oxygen out of the room! Somebody procured a beverage for her and people began to approach her, almost in the fashion of a receiving line. She saw Bill Cole and walked up to him and gave him a hug and a kiss on his cheek. She didn't do this to anyone else that I saw during the time I was in her presence. While others waited to speak to her, I was introduced.

Mrs. Irene Bolam was a most unusual woman for a number of reasons. First and foremost, she was a very elegant lady, refined and cultured. She appeared to be about the same age (70s) as my grandmother and was the same height as my sister. Mrs. Bolam stood about five feet eight inches. Her hair was very well styled and her suit was what one would expect of a lawyer or banker. She wore an Army Air Corps "wings and prop" insignia pinned to the left lapel of her jacket. Other than a string of pearls, she wore no other insignia or emblems that I recall. I think I asked her if her pearls were Mikimoto's. I don't' remember if she answered. (My mother had a Mikimoto pearl necklace.) Mrs. Bolam recognized and addressed me by my rank. She also recognized my aviator wings and asked me what types of aircraft I was flying. I told her that I flew helicopters, in those days the Bell UH-ID (Huey). She also recognized the decorations I had been awarded and commented on several of them.

I asked Mrs. Bolam what she had flown and she didn't answer. I asked her if she had flown a helicopter and she told me that she had never flown a helicopter, but once flew an autogiro. She then asked me if I knew what it was and of course I did. I asked her a question about the autogiro and she abruptly changed the subject by asking me where I had gone to College, I had attended the University of Kansas and informed her of this. She said, "Ah yes, Lawrence, a nice college town."

She asked about my family and I told her that my family was from Valley Falls, Kansas. She said, "Valley Falls, did you ever know a veterinarian named Foster, Dr. Irving Foster, I think?"

I told her, yes, that Irving Foster was my great grandfather and that he had died when I was a toddler. His practice took him throughout both Jefferson and Atchison counties. She changed the subject again to aviation. I was impressed at the depth of her knowledge. Her knowledge was "hands-on" knowledge. She demonstrated a "propeller hub to tail wheel" knowledge of flying.

She asked me if I was instrument rated and I told her yes, but most of my flying was VFR, because of the nature of Army Aviation's mission of close air support, troop insertion and re-supply of forward units. She was very aware of our aviation mission and demonstrated her knowledge in our conversation. She knew about the Army's plans for the Advanced Attack Helicopter, which eventually came on-line as the AH-64 Apache.

I spoke with her for about twenty minutes. Then Bill Cole mentioned that I should make my exit so others could speak with Irene. No doubt they were clamoring to do so. She told Bill to call her so that they could meet for lunch someday, as "It's been too long."

Mrs. Bolam controlled the conversation from start to finish. She was a woman accustomed to "running the show." However, she did it in a professional respectful way and with great skill. She certainly gave me every indication that she was interested in what I had to say about Army aviation, but she clearly knew more about it than just about any woman of her age and social status. She also mentioned some of the names of senior Army aviation leaders at the time, including the General Officer who commanded Ft. Rucker, Alabama.

I had mentioned that I would be leaving soon for Tokyo, then going on to Korea. She told me that Tokyo was a wonderful city and that I should make a point to visit and see some of the sights. She obviously had been there at some point in time and had a thorough knowledge of Japanese culture. She mentioned the Imperial Gardens and I did eventually visit this site. It really was breathtaking, just as she had said.

When we left the reception, Bill Cole told me, "Some people think that Irene is Amelia Earhart." I don't recall exactly what I said, but it was something like, "Yeah, sure, Bill." After all, I had been taught that Amelia Earhart died in 1937.

I only knew that I had met a very remarkable woman who clearly was the principal attendee at the old aviator's reception. For years I wondered just who she was and still am not sure. There are many unanswered questions about Irene Craigmile Bolam that nobody has been able to answer to my satisfaction.

I returned to my hotel room and left Newark the next morning for San Francisco. I then met my Port of Call at Travis Air Force Base and flew to Tokyo and after spending the night there, flew on to Seoul, Korea. From there I served my tour of duty in the Second Infantry Division's Second Aviation Company. I never saw Mrs. Bolam or Bill Cole again. He died in 1995, two years after my dad.

When I looked for information about Bill Cole, it seemed as if he never existed. A member of the Amelia Earhart Society has ridiculed my story and refers to Bill as the "so-called Bill Cole." He has so much as called me a liar regarding anything I've stated about Irene C. Bolam, Pratt & Whitney engines, etc. What I have to share obviously doesn't agree with his research.

Burkert's story continues with information about Bill Cole, who did exist and has an interesting story of his own.

In 1935, he was a twenty-one year old assembler at the Pratt and Whitney engine works. He was lucky to have a job at all in 1935, yet he did. After the 1937 Luke Field incident in which Amelia Earhart crash-landed her Lockheed L-10, Pratt & Whitney received an order to build two R-1340 engines for Earhart's L-10. Pratt & Whitney Employees worked overtime to make the deadline for completion. Most worked with reduced pay as it was the Depression and they really wanted to keep their jobs. Bill Cole worked on the assembling of those engines and used to tell the story of how everyone was to take special care as the engines were for "Miss Earhart's ship." The engines were built, final testing was conducted and the engines were mounted on test stands and "run-in." Bill Cole was one of the technicians on duty during the "run-in." This is where he met Paul Mantz.

Bill Cole never said that the engines were "super-duper" engines, as aforementioned Earhart researcher has mocked. Cole only said that the crew was to use special care in the building of the engines, because of whom they were consigned to. Everyone was aware of Amelia Earhart's intention to resume her world flight.

Paul Mantz was suitably impressed with Bill Cole and asked him if he would be willing to do some travel for the purpose of performing maintenance on Earhart's engines. Bill was interested and Mantz was able to "borrow" him from Pratt & Whitney, along with some other employees for her scheduled maintenance near the "halfway point." I don't know what "point" that was as I don't recall Bill ever saying. Some "island" is all I remember.

After July 1937, Bill Cole returned home to the USA. He never returned to Pratt & Whitney. He was able to enlist in the Army Air Forces with Paul Mantz's assistance. He also was able to enter the Army's Aviation Cadet Program without the requisite of two years of college.

Oddly enough, I really don't know much about Bill Cole. He was always a "shadowy" figure during my boyhood. He would appear from time to time, usually when he was between wives. Col. Rollin Reineck (Air Forces navigator and author of *Amelia Earhart Lives*) knew who he was, but didn't know him personally. Reineck was not yet a pilot at the time Bill left the Air Force. Also, Reineck was not aware of Bill's connection with Irene C. Bolam either.

I only became involved in this controversy as a result of a program on German television in 2005. I was stationed in Mannheim at the time and one of my German employees told me of the television program. It mentioned Rollin Reineck's book *Amelia Earhart Lives*.

I did some research and found the book and publisher. I contacted Douglas Westfall and told him of my having met Irene C. Bolam in 1977. This got me in contact with Col. Reineck and ultimately with Irene E. Bolam, with whom I have corresponded on a regular basis during the past nine months. (This Irene is the wife of John Bolam, whose older brother was Guy Bolam, Irene C. Bolam's husband.)

Essentially, the above is, to the best of my recollection, what I recall about my meeting with Mrs. Bolam. I did not meet Guy Bolam, as he had died in 1970, before the time of the Newark reception. I only learned of this near Christmas 2005.

I have been asked if I think Irene C. Bolam was Amelia Earhart. I don't know the answer to this question. If she wasn't, she certainly was a "dead ringer" for Amelia Earhart. I saw her and the photographs are accurate. The so-called Gervais/Irene is the lady I met and spoke with. I have no idea who the others are or were.

I thank Michael Burkert for allowing me to include his report in this book. What he had to say about his chance meeting with Irene C. Bolam was similar to mine and could be probably repeated numerous times with other people who have had those experiences and shared them.

My chance meeting with Irene C. Bolam happened after attending a 50th wedding anniversary for my wife's cousin. A group of us were invited to Irene C. Bolam's house, which I did not know. While I was driving there, my wife's other cousin, whom we had brought to the celebration, leaned over and quietly told me that Irene was thought to be Amelia Earhart. I was not prepared for what happened next, as I was just the designated driver.

During the cocktail party, I was looking at many photographs, mostly of groups, in sitting room off to one side. With a drink in hand, Irene came in carrying a cocktail for me. She didn't appear upset at finding me looking at the photographs, but may have thought I knew more than I did. Perhaps my wife and her cousins had told her I was a pilot, because she started talking about her flying days. I don't remember everything she told me, but she made two points very clear. One was that she was one of the early women flyers and two that she had received the third flying license issued to a woman. After reading Fred Goerner's book, I think I figured out what she was telling me. Amelia was very smart, she had a mathematical mind and loved word games and codes. I think she was trying to tell me that she flew in the FIRST Powder Puff Derby and came in THIRD. Thus may be a stretch, but it is the best I could come up with at the time. She certainly was not going to tell me that she was Amelia Earhart.

I suppose that it can be documented whether or not Irene C. Bolam, earlier known as Craigmile was a rated pilot and the type of aircraft she flew identified in her logbook.

I've learned some new things from other Earhart researchers. None, however, have persuaded me toward accepting any of the other theories regarding the 1937 disappearance. The entire Irene Craigmile Bolam scenario seems to me a "conspiracy of silence," a phrase I didn't originate. I believe there is a concerted effort to dismiss the research conducted by Joe Gervais as published in Joe Klaas' book *Amelia Earhart Lives*. Additionally, the "experts" have summarily dismissed the research and the documentation provided by Rollin Reineck and Tod Swindell. Why?

During the last few years of her life, Irene suffered from bone cancer. Knowing that she was ill, she had time to plan what was to happen after her death. She planned her Memorial Service, choosing October 29, 1982, the anniversary date of her mother Amy's death. She also chose the menu. The invited guests included her granddaughter and the biological son of the first Irene O'Crowley Craigmile.

Amelia did have a problem, however, which was going to be difficult to solve. She had been using the name Irene Craigmile, a real person for 37 years and Irene Bolam for 24 years. Craigmile was a cover name taken from a real person, Irene O'Crowley Craigmile, to allow her to return to the United States. Irene really was Amelia Earhart and that was the name she was going to use. That meant there could be no public gravesite.

When Gervais was doing his research, he discovered a secret agreement between the United States and Japan that no representative would talk about the Amelia Earhart story while she was still living. Yet, silence still reigns on the part of both nations well after her death. This is disservice to both Amelia Earhart and Fred Noonan while they are hidden in their secret "graves." The time is right that both receive public burials so that people in this country and Japan can choose to come and honor them.

Her solution was to go to her birthplace in Atchison, Kansas. It had to be a secret burial site. Thus, she was put in the cellar of that home, where she is today, under a sheath of copper mesh and concrete. Later on, Fred Noonan, who had a similar situation, was also placed there.

Maybe the reason I just happened to see that photo of Amelia that day at the YMCA was because there was a sense she wanted to be taken out of the cellar where she is. She had to feel that the time was right for her to have a public grave where people from around the world could visit.

I suggest a plan to accomplish what I believe Amelia Earhart would like to happen. I have spent thousands of hours researching her story and have tried to tell it to you as best as I can. I have visited her gravesite and in my judgment, it is a disgrace. Here is the most famous woman of her time and known throughout the world put away in a cellar because WWII is not over yet. The Japanese might be offended if the truth were known.

I have shared what I believe to be the truth in this book for all to read and contemplate. Shall we do nothing or do we help Amelia Earhart have a public gravesite known to everyone? Why not give her a proper gravesite? President Roosevelt is buried at Hyde Park in New York State for all to visit and yet he was involved in repulsive activities.

Various aviation groups, interested individuals, international service clubs and corporations worldwide could fund the monument. Knowing what really happened in 1937, coupled with what finally happened to Amelia, might draw their interest.

If not do it for Amelia, then what about for the millions of young women who began to fly after reading about Amelia Earhart. How many future pilots and astronauts are out there who might do the same thing after learning what Earhart accomplished during her stellar flying career?

# AFTERWORD

The idea that history should be as it was and told that way has led me to write this book. There is no way the entire history of Amelia Earhart's last flight and its aftermath can be written. The manuscript would be too long and involve thousands of people and the parts they played in the saga.

What can be done, however, is now that the basic facts of her last flight are known and people read about the plight she was placed in, they can begin to understand her actions during the flight, rescue and later while she was in Japan. Her country left her to die, alone and helpless on an island. This led to her participation in activities in Japan that she probably would have stayed away from had circumstances been different.

Thus, should she be forgiven considering what happened to thousands in the world as a result of her actions? Should she forever be remembered for these acts and not for what she had done before that final flight? In order for someone to be forgiven, one has to know what that person had done to need forgiveness. It is known what she did during and after her flight. Now it is up to individuals to decide whether the final judgment should be based on those deeds. Or, should she be forgiven for what happened when she was placed in a situation no one would have dared to imagine. It is up to the American people to decide.

Amelia Earhart and Fred Noonan's grave at Amelia's Birthplace in Atchison, Kansas. Pictures taken by Suzanne Bower in July 2012.

Amelia Earhart's grave.

# REFERENCES

Beck, Glenn. (2013). *The Making of America, Miracles and Massacres – True & Untold Stories*. New York, New York: Threshold Editions/Mercury Radio Arts.

Beckman, Allan. (1982). *Niihau Incident*. Honolulu, HI: Heritage Press of Pacific.

Bergamini, David. (1971). *Japan's Conspiracy – How Hirohito Led Japan Into War Against the West*. New York, New York: William Morrow and Company.

Briand Jr., Paul. (1960). *Daughter of the Sky*. New York, New York: Duell, Sloan and Pearce.

Brink, Randal. (1995). *Lost Star: The Search for Amelia Earhart*. New York, New York: W.W. Norton & Company.

Bryan Jr., E.H.. (1974) *Panala'au Memoirs*. Honolulu, HI: Pacific Science Information Center/Bernice P. Bishop Museum.

Burlingame, Burl. (1992). *Advance Force – Pearl Harbor*. Annapolis, MD: Naval Institute Press.

Cochran, Jackie. (1954). *The Stars at Noon*. Boston, Massachusetts: Little, Brown and Company.

Earhart, Amelia. (1937). *Last Flight*. New York, New York: Harcourt, Brace & World, Inc.

Gauvreau, Emile. (1944). *The Wild Blue Yonder*. New York, New York: E.P. Dutton & Company, Inc.

Griffin, W.E.B. & Butterworth IV, William E.. (2010). *The Outlaws: A Presidential Agent Novel*. New York, New York: G.P. Putnam's Sons (Penguin Group).

Goerner, Fred. (1966). *The Search for Amelia Earhart*. Garden City, New York: Doubleday & Company, Inc.

Hoyt, Edwin P. (2001). *Yamamoto, The Man Who Planned the Attack on Pearl Harbor*. Guilford, Connecticut: The Lyons Press.

Kaucher, Dorothy. (1947). *Wings Over Wake*. San Francisco, California: John Howell.

Kennedy, Art. (1992). *High Times*. Santa Barbara, California: Fithian Press.

Klass, Joe. (2000). *Amelia Earhart Lives*. Lincoln, NE: iUniverse.com, Inc..

Loomis, Vincent. (1985). *Amelia Earhart, The Final Story*. New York: Random House.

Myers, Robert. (1985). *Stand By to Die*. Pacific Grove, California: Lighthouse Writer's Guild.

Persico, Joseph. (2001). *Roosevelt's Secret War*. New York, New York: Random House.

Reinbeck, Rollin C.. (2003). *Amelia Earhart Survived*. Orange, California: The Paragon Agency.

Stinnett, Robert. (2000). *Day of Deceit*. New York, New York: Touchstone.

Toland, John. (1982). *Infamy: Pearl Harbor and Its Aftermath.* Garden City, New York: Doubleday & Company, Inc.

Willey, Mark Emerson. (2000). *Pearl Harbor – Mother of All Conspiracies.* Bloomington, IN: Xlibris Corporation (Author Solutions).

## MAGAZINES

Palmer, Charles. (1942, November). "Was Amelia Earhart the War's First Casualty?". *Skyways Magazine,* Vol. 1, No. 1.

Article in the *Nassau Daily News,* Freeport, NY.

## RESEARCH FILES

The Paul Briand papers. Ezekiel W. Dimond Library Special Collections. University of New Hampshire, Durham.

The Joe Gervais papers. Eugene McDermott Library Special Collections. University of Texas, Richardson.